Jumpstart
Your _____, Vol III

15 Inspiring Entrepreneurs Share Stories and
Strategies on How to Jumpstart Many Areas of Your
Life, Business, Relationships, and Health

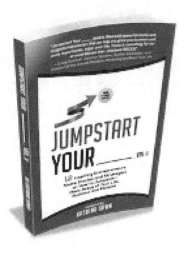

Compiled by Katrina Sawa
*CEO & Founder of JumpstartYourBusinessNow.com
and JumpstartPublishing.net*

D1596247

Get to Know the 15 Inspiring Authors in this Book!

There's ONE page online where you can access all the authors' websites and special offers from this book to make it super easy for you to follow up and connect with them further.

Go to www.JumpstartBookAuthors.com right now before you forget. For a list of authors and their chapters, turn to the Table of Contents page.

Katrina Sawa, Speaker, Best-Selling Author, Award-Winning Business & Marketing Coach to Entrepreneurs Who Want More LOVE in Their Lives and MONEY in Their Businesses!

Published by K. Sawa Marketing International Inc. PO Box 6, Roseville, CA 95661. (916) 872-4000 www.JumpstartPublishing.net

DISCLAIMER AND/OR LEGAL NOTICES

While all attempts have been made to verify information provided in this book and its ancillary materials, neither the authors nor publisher assume any responsibility for errors, inaccuracies, or omissions and are not responsible for any financial loss by customer in any manner. Any slights of people or organizations are unintentional. If advice concerning legal, financial, accounting or related matters is needed, the services of a qualified professional should be sought. This book and its associated ancillary materials, including verbal and written training, are not intended for use as a source of legal, financial or accounting advice. You should be aware of the various laws governing business transactions or other business practices in your particular geographical location.

EARNINGS & INCOME DISCLAIMER

With respect to the reliability, accuracy, timeliness, usefulness, adequacy, completeness, and/or suitability of information provided in this book, Katrina Sawa, K. Sawa Marketing International Inc., its partners, associates, affiliates, consultants, and/or presenters make no warranties, guarantees, representations, or claims of any kind. Readers' results will vary. Any and all claims or representations as to income earnings are not to be considered as average earnings. This book and all products and services are for educational and informational purposes only. Check with your accountant, attorney or professional advisor before acting on this or any information. Katrina Sawa and/or K. Sawa Marketing International Inc. is not responsible for the success or failure of your business, personal, health or financial decisions relating to any information presented by Katrina Sawa, K. Sawa Marketing International Inc., or company products/services.

Any examples, stories, reference, or case studies are for illustrative purposes only and should not be interpreted as testimonies and/or examples of what readers and/or consumers can generally expect from the information. Any statements, strategies, concepts, techniques, exercises and ideas in the information, materials and/or seminar training offered are simply opinion or experience, and thus should not be misinterpreted as promises, typical results or guarantees (expressed or implied).

ISBN: 978-1-7358666-1-1

PRINTED IN THE UNITED STATES OF AMERICA

Dedication

This book is dedicated to Entrepreneurs everywhere who have the desire and mission to make a bigger impact with those they serve.

Here's to creating and enjoying the business and life of your dreams!

Special thank you to my husband Jason and step-daughter Riley who support me 100% on all of my entrepreneurial endeavors. And thank you to all of the awesome jumpstart authors.

Praise for the Jumpstart Your _____ Books

Are you ready to Jumpstart your 2020?

"This is the perfect time for this book to come out. I'm so glad I bought this! So many incredible stories of ways to jumpstart your business, your love life, your dreams, anything you can think of. These are my favorite books to read. I definitely recommend this book!" - Candi & Sean Douglas

Great read -- Short doses of inspiration

"This is a great book. Many tidbits of motivation. You can read any chapter and gain inspiration to take on the day's challenges. I love the stories and perspectives provided." - Karen T. Peak

Another great book by Katrina Sawa & Friends

"Katrina Sawa always brings her readers beneficial info for growing a business in the current marketplace." - PK Odle

Excellent Co-Authors with a variety of backgrounds

"Really great content, the authors here have a variety of backgrounds which is great for insight!" - Matt Brauning

A Great Source of Inspiration!

"Being an Entrepreneur is a really tough... but rewarding job! Sometimes you need a little extra encouragement to push you through the rough times. This is an incredible book, packed with all kinds of inspiring entrepreneur stories. I found nuggets of wisdom and inspiration all at the same time!" - Richard B. Greene

Katrina Sawa Never Disappoints

"Katrina Sawa never disappoints when she is delivering information to her audience of fans and she certainly delivers with her latest book. Thank you, Katrina, for gathering this group of experts to provide us with a great resource." - RL Escobar-Balcom

There is something for Everyone!

"Jumpstart Your _____ is filled with powerful stories and insightful takeaways that can help you grow your business and more importantly, enjoy your life. There is something for everyone! Bottom line - this book ROCKS!" - Craig Duswalt, Keynote Speaker, Author, Podcaster, and Creator of the brands RockStar Marketing and Rock Your Life.

So much great Inspiration!

"Hard to believe so much great information is available in ONE book. Whatever you dream... you can achieve! You are bound to find something impactful in this book!" - Marguerite Crespillo

Table of Contents

Jumpstart Your Business Chapters

Introduction

This book, *Jumpstart Your _____, Volume III*, is for you if you need a jumpstart in any areas of your life, career, business, mindset, health, relationships, beliefs, and more!

This is the third book in the *Jumpstart Your _____* series, and we keep getting new, fresh topics, content, and authors! This volume has 14 new authors in addition to myself. We have a wide variety this time, with advice for the parent, caregiver, and business owner, as well as the person who wants to improve his or her life, health, and even relationship with a pet or significant other. It's fun to see who comes through with each book, and what expertise they bring.

The authors with whom I have collaborated on this book are experts in their industries and in what they teach. Our goal is to provide a book that shows you how and why you should consider jumpstarting many of the areas covered within these chapters.

If you enjoy any one or more of the stories and chapters within this book, please reach out and contact the author(s). They want to know that their chapter encouraged you, inspired you, or motivated you in some way. They also want to know how they can help you. Each author has provided some kind of next step or free gift at the end of their chapter, to give you the opportunity to learn more. Don't stop with this book: please take the initiative and reach out for more information, more help, and more advice for whatever you might be trying to jumpstart in your life right now. Who knows: maybe after your initial read-through of this book, you will pick it up a couple years from now and decide to jump start something else.

This edition of *Jumpstart Your_____* can help literally anyone, I believe. There are chapters you'll find immediately helpful, and some you may not need until years from now--but keep it handy just in case, because you never know!

Half of the chapters in this book will help you jumpstart an area of your personal life, and half of them are geared more towards helping business owners. Whether or not you have a business, one day you may! Order extra copies of these books for friends, family, or clients; they will appreciate your thoughtfulness.

What about you? Do you have an area of expertise about which you could write in one of our Jumpstart Your _____ books? One thing I know to be true is that most entrepreneurs really do need a book in this day and age. You need to be an author to really be seen as the expert in your industry, or even in the company for which you work. Writing a whole book by yourself is a lot of work, takes a lot of time, and sometimes costs a lot of money. Being an author in a compilation book like this one, however, is a lot less cumbersome, less stressful, and less costly. It's also helpful when somebody puts it all together for you, and you don't have to worry about all the details of editing, cover design, proofing, and publishing. (That's what we do here at Jumpstart Publishing.)

I've been in business since 2002. I've been an author in ten compilation books, plus two of my own full-length books. I have put together this opportunity to become a published author, with very little effort and work on your part--if you're interested. Contact us if you might be interested in being an author in the next *Jumpstart Your* _____ book, and share your story!

And if you've ever thought about starting, growing, or marketing your own business, and/or becoming an author or speaker, please reach out to me; I'm extremely passionate about helping anybody build a profitable business doing what they love. - Katrina Sawa

Jumpstart Your Life/ Self Chapters

Jumpstart Your Best Life

5 Tips to Living out Your Dreams

By Emily Yatsko Sandusky

When was the last time you allowed yourself to dream? I mean, really dream: those wild, outlandish dreams where you allow your mind to keep going and do not let the fear of failure kick in?

Will you humor me and allow yourself to dream in this moment? Think back to when you were a kid and your imagination would run wild about what you would be when you grew up! Anything was possible.

I have some questions for you to ask yourself every few years, to make sure you are on the path to living the life you want and going after your dreams. I want to ensure that you're still focused on living out your best life. Don't ever settle for less than what you truly desire. You get one shot, one life! You are meant to do extraordinary things!

Questions to get you thinking:

- What if I could be/do/have anything?

- If I had the time AND the money, what would I be doing?

- What if I didn't know how many days I had left to live?
  - Would I be living my life differently?
  - Would I shift my priorities?
  - Would I act differently?
  - Would I show up differently? More confidently, perhaps? More purposefully? More intentionally?
  - Would I spend less time worrying about what other people think?
  - Would I spend more time with the people I love?
  - Would I be kinder?
  - Would I be quicker to forgive myself and others?
  - Would I love more?
  - Would I push past my fears and my limiting beliefs?
  - Would I stop worrying about the fear of failing?

The truth is that we only have one life to live. Our life is made up of moments: days, weeks, months, years.

I am a four-time cancer survivor. I was first diagnosed with Leukemia when I was 5 years old. I didn't understand the severity of what that meant. I just knew it meant a lot of "pokes" and throwing up. The perk was that I got to miss school, pick out chips from the vending machine, and get a lot of stuffed animals and extra attention. After two years of chemotherapy, I went into remission. When I was 11 years old, I relapsed. I was mortified to lose my hair as a middle schooler. I hated being different and missing sports and friends. I did my best to continue with as much normalcy as possible when I felt strong enough. I kept going to school, and I even planned my chemo around tests. I did two more years of chemo, and once again went into remission. When I was 17 years old, about to be a starter on the varsity soccer team, l relapsed again. This time, it really felt like my world was crumbling around me. I was playing the best soccer of my life, was surrounded by incredible friends and loving life...and then this: cancer! I was angry, frustrated and disappointed.

"Really? Why does this keep happening to me? Haven't I had enough?" I asked God.

Quickly, I realized that feeling sorry for myself wasn't going to help anything. After intense chemo, I had a stem cell transplant. Miraculously, my brother was a perfect match. My body accepted the transplant, I went into remission, and I built up a whole new immune system. Even when I got to go back to school, it was hard. My body wasn't as strong as it was before.

Then, I got into college at my dream school, Northwestern University, and I couldn't wait. I was so ready to start fresh, meet new people, be on my own, and start a new chapter of my life. The first 2 quarters of college were amazing. I was loving life. I was totally in my element. Then, it happened: I started to feel intense pain in my hips, and I knew it was back. Just before the end of my freshman year in college, I relapsed again.

I couldn't believe it! I really couldn't believe it. Why did this cancer keep coming back? Why, just when I began to feel one of my euphoric highs, did it immediately get ripped away? It didn't seem fair.

Two more years of chemo, and I was back in remission. This time was different. I got an infection in my face that quickly spread throughout my body, and ended with emergency surgery in the middle of the night to stop it. Another time, I had a reaction to a medication that caused severe diarrhea, and I lost 30 pounds. Another time, I had a neurological reaction to a medication that left me without memories from a whole week of my life.

Thankfully, I'm still around to tell my story, but the reality is that we don't know what's ahead or how many days we have left. My whole childhood taught me this lesson. I realized that I needed to live every day like it was my last. I needed to work every day to show up in the world as my best self.

These lessons trickled down to my family and friends. I know now that I am here for a bigger purpose. I'm here to tell my story so that you can wake up and start making the positive life changes that YOU need to make in order to start living your dream, one small step at a time.

How do you want to be remembered? Why not start being your best self, so that you can start living your best life today?

5 tips for being your best self so you can start living your best life:

1. **Create a morning practice** – It can include meditation, prayer, affirmations, reading personal growth books, and other practices. What makes YOU feel good? Fill your tank first thing every day, before checking your email, visiting social media, or even helping your children; it's so important. It will impact how you show up, respond to, and interact with everything and everyone else.

2. **Beyond your morning routine, think about other daily, weekly, and monthly self-care practices** - What are you doing to take care of yourself? We all need proper nutrition, exercise, sleep, and hydration in order to feel our best. What areas have you been neglecting that you can add back in?

3. **Visualize who you want to be, and what you want your life to look like** - Start by making a list of 100 things you want to do/be/have. Read that list and visualize it as if those things have already happened--every day. What does it feel like, look like, sound like, and smell like? Who is there with you? Review it, add to it, check off things you've accomplished, and celebrate those accomplishments!

4. **Surround yourself with the right people** - Make a list of 5 people who encourage you, cheer you on, inspire you, and want you to succeed.

Schedule time to be around them as much as possible. Schedule lunches, outings, date nights, get-togethers, or phone calls to fill your spirit with positive energy and encouragement for living your best life. Also, make another list of people who bring you down, cause drama in your life, or say/do harmful things to you. Have a conversation with them, and take the time to figure out whether you simply need to set healthy boundaries with them, or whether they even belong in your life at all.

5. **Keep a positive attitude and perspective** - How you show up every day is your choice. Before you get out of bed in the morning, decide how you are going to show up. Choose to see things through a lens of love, not fear. You won't always be perfect, of course, but you can be better every day. The more you commit to this, the easier it will get. This includes how you talk to and treat yourself, love and respect yourself. You are amazing, worthy, able, perfect, and complete. You are lovable and beautiful. You deserve to live your best life, and to achieve your dream life!

Today, I live in Colorado with my husband Ryan and identical twin boys, Mason and Gryffin. I have the happiest life I can possibly imagine for myself. Is it perfect? Of course not. However, I strive every day to live my best life, to find joy, to go after my dreams, and to be grateful for the life I have been given and the lessons I have learned along the way.

I am grateful that I get to help people go after their dreams and live their best lives. I have been an Independent Consultant with Arbonne International for 10 years. We embrace the holistic approach to health and wellness: a healthy mind, body, and skin are all connected, and they are the foundation for being your best self so that you can live your best life.

If you want to know more about this community, the products, and the business as a channel for creating your best life, let me know. I would love to help you jump start your best life!

Every month, I hold a drawing for new subscribers to my website, so head over to www. EmilySanduskyBestLife.com and enter to win!

About the Author
Emily Yatsko Sandusky

Emily is a 4x cancer survivor with a degree in Human Development and Psychological Services from Northwestern University and a Masters in Special Education from the University of Colorado. Emily is a former Special Education teacher, author of Hope Triumphs ALL, and an independent consultant with a holistic health, skin, and beauty company, Arbonne International. Emily lives in Colorado with her husband Ryan and identical twins Mason and Gryffin.

Jumpstart Your Caregiving Skills

The Secret to Less Stress When Caregiving

By Toni Gitles

Your phone rings. It's the hospital emergency room admissions desk. They found your contact information in your dad's wallet. You are bombarded with questions about his medical history, medications, allergies, and physician contact information.

You are stunned. You ask, "Is he going to be O.K.?" Your mind is racing. You gasp for air. Do you really want to tell the nurse you don't know this information? Do you have time to race to your parents' home and look for this information?

This scenario happens more often than you can imagine. An accident or health issue occurs, and boom! Not only does the life of the family member change in an instant, but the person who will care for him or her is completely blindsided. Suddenly, a son or daughter becomes a caregiver. In life, we are told, "Expect the best and prepare for the worst." We are good at the former, but pretty bad at the latter.

It Did Happen to Me

An attitude that "this can't happen to me" is useless.

In March 2006, at age 89, my mom was hospitalized with a life-threatening illness. At one point, the neurologist warned me, "I'm sorry, but *if* your mom survives, she will never be able to live independently again. You'd better prepare." With those words, and the fact that she *did* survive, my life changed. For the next 12 years until her passing in February 2017, my time and energy were focused on caring for Mom.

The Secret Every Caregiver Figures Out... Eventually

Although Mom's legal and healthcare documents were in order, this hospitalization showed me how ill-prepared I was to guide my mother through the healthcare system and manage her multiple illnesses. I struggled to define and assume my role as her primary caregiver. Not only did I need to communicate with my mother about her healthcare, but I also became the one to communicate and advocate for her with doctors, nurses, and assisted living staff.

I only found out later that this experience can change your life in a most positive and life-affirming way. And the best kept secret? The distress and stress are less if you don't try to do it all by yourself, and caregiving does not have to rob you of your health and sanity in the process.

You Can Have A Less Stressed, More Informed, and More Supported Experience

I started my company, Heart Light Enterprises, specifically to help individuals and families navigate the entire caregiving experience from the early preparation phase, through the "overwhelm" of the crisis stage, and on to starting again when caregiving ends.

One thing every new caregiver learns is that during a crisis is not the optimal time to figure things out. NOW is the time to jumpstart your caregiving skills with proven guidelines, whether you anticipate caring for a loved one in the future, or whether you have already begun your caregiving journey.

The Three Tips to Getting Support as a Caregiver

Tip # 1: Preparation and Planning

Preparing and planning now will save time, energy, and regrets later.

When my dad died unexpectedly in 1989, Mom directed me to a file cabinet in the house where Dad had organized and labeled all his important documents. During this incredible time of grief, not having to search the house for the essential paperwork was a welcome relief. It also served to inform us to organize and update documents for Mom so I could easily access this information when needed. At the same time, I updated my documents as well, realizing that anyone, anytime, can have a health crisis and need someone to care for them.

This is a brief overview of what's included in the Care Plans I custom-design for each of my clients, to get you started.

- Legal Planning. Make sure that wills are written and/or updated. The assignment of a durable power of attorney (DPOA) delegates the power to whomever you choose to legally handle your affairs in case you are disabled or incapacitated. Without a DPOA, no one may be able to access bank accounts, insurance records, securities, and property without lengthy and expensive legal proceedings. An advance directive explains how you want medical decisions about you to be made if you cannot make the decisions yourself, and designates an individual who can be proactive in making healthcare decisions for you.

- Medical Planning. Keep a list of current medications and allergies. Create a health history document, including past diagnoses and surgical procedures. Know where health and life insurance records, and prepaid funeral contracts, are kept.

- Financial Records. Know the bank name and account numbers, investment account records, and where checkbooks and the safety deposit box are kept. Know Social Security information.

- Personal Information. Create a contact list of family and friends.

In my practice, adult children often say they don't want their parents talking to them about final arrangements and personal information. Also, parents may not want to burden their children with this information. If either of these situations sounds familiar, plan to start this conversation RIGHT now. If you can't talk about it, plant the seed with your loved ones to leave an organized notebook of relevant information, and let you know where to find it.

Without a DPOA and these necessary, up-to-date documents, your loved ones will be left with a very stressful situation and you don't want to do that to them, do you? And if YOU are the potential caregiver, you don't want your parent or spouse to leave YOU with a big mess to figure out either, so you've got to get them on board with this, regardless of how stubborn or in denial they are.

Tip #2: Education and Information

Educate yourself, because knowledge gives you power now and later.

Most of us only have a vague idea of what it means to be a caregiver and what the responsibilities will be. There is an abundance of information to learn about the stages of caregiving, such as:

- Understanding the illness or disease progression
- Managing emergency room and hospital visits
- Interaction with healthcare professionals
- How to give hands-on care

Especially in the case of dementia, there are the ongoing grief and emotions that accompany the deterioration of a family member.

Being informed allows you to find joy in the good times, savor the moments, and end the journey with no regrets.

Tip #3: Support

Between emergency room, hospital, doctor visits, and taking care of yourself, caregiving can easily turn into a 24/7 job. The only child or key sibling who has no help and believes "I'm the only one who can do this the right way!" is headed for exhaustion, stress, and their own health crisis.

Find support and learn to ask for help. You *may* be the best positioned to care for your loved one, but you are not the *only* one to provide care. This can be an incredibly isolating experience. Please don't take this journey alone.

Ways you can get support include:

- Set up a team of helpers with your family and friends, and decide ahead of time what help they are willing to provide. Usually having a list of tasks available is helpful.

- Consider hiring a home companion or a skilled in-home provider. Certified Caregiving Consultants™ can be there for *you* through your entire caregiving experience.

- Consider joining a support group where other caregivers share their experiences, resources, and understand exactly the range of emotions you go through each day.

A Final Heartfelt Thought

Life is about love. We are here to have loving relationships. Approach caregiving from your heart, from a place of unconditional love for your care recipient, and accept and appreciate the gift of taking care of them and being there when they take their final breath on earth.

Despite the hardships and challenges of caregiving, I eventually realized that taking care of Mom was to be the most meaningful and positive life-altering experience of my life. My biggest wish was that I would have done more planning, had more information, more support, and an avenue to address and release the overwhelming extent of emotions that seems to go hand-in-hand with caring for a loved one.

I know from experience the value of these caregiving skills, and want to ease your stress.

I created a special webpage at www. MyCaregiverConsultant.com/jumpstart for you to grab a free copy of my Caregiving Guidebook: The 21 Mistakes Caregivers Make and How to Avoid Them. It will help you jumpstart or continue your caregiving experience with more ease. It includes more detail about the topics in this chapter, plus the following:

• Prepare to Care Pre-Planning Checklist

• Caregiver Assessment

• Resources for Caregivers

Here's to a caregiving experience filled with peace of mind and ease!

About the Author
Toni Gitles

Toni Gitles is an International Speaker, co-author of *Happiness is a Decision of the Heart*, Certified Caregiving Consultant™, Educator™, and Trained Dementia Practitioner. She is passionate about providing support for family caregivers and would be honored to help you navigate your caregiving experience from early preparation through the overwhelm of the caregiving journey in order to decrease your stress and to help you find meaning, resilience and joy from this life-changing event.

Jumpstart Your Exponential Prosperity

Propel Yourself Through the 7 Energetic Levels of Money!

By Susan Glusica

Abundant prosperity is your birthright. Just by breathing, you are worthy of plentitude, surplus, and overflow--and lots of money!

Does that idea create resistance for you? Then perhaps you are a prisoner of the middle-class mindset!

A middle-class mindset is one in which:

- Money comes in, and goes right back out.

- You have been taught that "money doesn't grow on trees," or

- If you get something you desire, it's because someone else didn't get what they wanted.

I remember being taught by my well-meaning parents that the Universe was limited. My sisters and I only got what we really wanted for Christmas every third year—we alternated, because there wasn't enough for all of us to have what we wanted every year. We shared everything!

We humans are designed to replicate our environment, so it was no surprise that I followed in my mother's footprints, got a secretarial certificate, and worked on Wall Street at a major private brokerage firm.

Twenty years later, having reached the self-imposed cap of my earning capacity, I had a crisis of legacy. I couldn't see my footprint. My soul cried out for full expression!

I moved from the "corporate cubicle" side of the industry to the client-facing side, to make a greater impact on my own life and on the lives of others. After 8 years helping people with their financial plans, I realized that, no matter their income level (and I work with incomes from $100K to $1 million plus), *people don't know how to get, grow, and give more, so that they can be, do, and have more.*

Enter my signature discovery of the 7 Energetic Levels of Money Consciousness in 2018, birthed from my work with an amazing business strategist. I call them the 7 Money Realities™. I started a group coaching program to help decision makers and enterprising business leaders get more clarity and confidence when it comes to their money, and to help open them up to the unlimited opportunities in their world right now. I help power partners—in life or business or both—move forward to soul-fulfilling living and service.

Everything is energy.

Many people talk about having a "money mindset." While that's definitely important, what's essential is realizing that, before thought, we are energy. And so is money. If we want more money (or more of what money gives us), then we must be a vibrational match, or match the energetic frequency, for our desired level of money.

In his book, *Power vs. Force*, Sir David Hawkins created a Map of Consciousness, whereby one can calibrate the frequency of any given state of mind, or consciousness, in the human body. The range is from 0 (Death) to 1,000 (Krishna, Buddha, Jesus). Gratitude is the highest state in which a human can vibrate within the body, at 900. And as we go from 1 to 999, the energy exponentially increases.

Reading the book a second time, I realized that this is exactly how money operates. There are distinct levels of energy when it comes to money consciousness. And there are specific steps I have for my clients to help them move upward toward the ultimate goal of Enlightened Gratitude.

The higher we vibe, the greater the abundance we attract to our lives.

My favorite example to illustrate how this works is going from Level 4, Harmonious Acceptance, to Level 5, Loving Money. I had a client once tell me, "I hate money." Well, if I were money, I'd stay as far away from you as possible if you hated me. His negative mindset was costing this client a lot, in the form of missing out on what that money could've done for him. It was costing him sleepless nights, challenges in the dating scene, and the inability to expand his business, among other things. We shifted him quickly into the level of Loving Money.

Moving to a level where you love money is actually quite simple: Write a love letter to money. You see, we are taught (by our parents, society, the educational system, etc.) that to have money means we must work hard for it. That's quite masculine: the going after, the doing, the striving, the getting. Meanwhile, that leaves out the other half of the energetic equation, the feminine side of things.

So, writing a letter of love to money comes from the softer side. It comes from the part of you that woos. It comes from the side of you that attracts, invites, and makes welcome. It's where you hold space for what you want, space for what you're calling into being (a.k.a. birthing).

Let's take a quick step back. In order for you to receive what you want, you must know what you desire. Unless you do this on the regular, you usually don't know what you really, really want. It's ok to start with what you don't want, and then reverse engineer those ideas into what you do want. Once you have a clear picture of what you do want, figure out a clear picture of the money that will be necessary in order to have it. Permission is hereby granted for you to desire more!

As one of my clients told me, it's amazing how quickly we can spend money. She completed an exercise in which she "gave" herself some extra money, and it was spent as easily as she could spend on her current income level. She realized that she wasn't asking for enough, wasn't charging her value, and she changed that up immediately. In doing so, she instantly jumped a level in her money consciousness, and within 30 days, she added more than $8K to her world.

Another client has shared that she didn't realize how much the middle-class mindset was interfering with her ability to invite in and receive the money she wanted so that she and her husband could retire in 10 years. She knew something was in the way, and within 2 weeks of our work together in private sessions, she had to quadruple her monthly income goal! She had busted through to inviting in and welcoming money, she was in the flow, and she had already attained her original money goal. This is life-changing, when you realize what's been in your way and you shift into expanded money energy.

As I like to say, "There is nothing as generative as clarity."

We are multidimensional beings who have a human tendency to over-rely on our 5 physical senses. When we remember that we have other dimensions within ourselves, including energy and vibrational frequencies, and we know what to do to leverage these other dimensions to make the physical action easier—and by that, I mean a lever which enables us to go farther with less effort—we attain higher and higher levels of fulfillment, service to others, and money. And we benefit from all that comes with it!

I've had clients sell their houses for their ask price or better, in cash, by their established deadline! They typically double their income and attract the house of their dreams. The benefits of my counseling also tend to rub off on family members, who end up getting full scholarships, and more. It wasn't coincidental that, within a year and a half of my discovery, because I am a product of my process, that we had a $1 million plus household year, upleveled my car, moved into our ideal house, and expanded our land. In fact, we got "bonused" working hay fields and forest preserves, which deliver rabbits, multiple bird species including turkeys, deer, and a coyote for us to view outside our windows! We enjoy our land even more than we'd anticipated. In that same year, we also added a Mediterranean apartment to our lives, where we vacation yearly and visit with family.

I teach my clients how to have all this and more in their own lives: whatever it is they truly desire. If we operate from a place where there are unlimited opportunities to receive what we want, then the way is always present for whatever we do want.

Quick Pro Tip: To quickly and optimally Jumpstart Your Prosperity, find the smallest thing in your current situation for which you can be grateful. Remember, gratitude is the highest vibration we can embody. When we "vibe" gratitude, really turn it up and get into that energy, as often as possible, we become a vibrational match to whatever it is that we want out of life.

Another avenue you can pursue is to have a coach show you how to manifest this successful life for yourself, so you save the time of figuring it out on your own with trial and error. If you're interested in exploring this, please schedule a call with me. I have a series of questions designed to get you crystal clear on what's possible for your prosperity, and whether what I offer can help actualize the potential inherent in your being. I look forward to being of service to you! Just go to my website at www.SusanGlusica. com/jumpstart and you'll have an opportunity to sign up for a call with me, and I'll also share a video exercise to get you going on your prosperity journey.

About the Author
Susan Glusica

Susan is the UNRIVALED REALIZER, known for humanizing the fastest path to inviting in and receiving more money because she is a stand for UNAPOLOGETIC PROSPERITY. Susan created the 7 Money Realities program, providing a powerfully practical method for attracting and realizing more money. She is an International Best-Selling author, a Lifetime Member and Certified Speaker of Women's Prosperity Network, and she is involved in multiple organizations, including Polka Dot Powerhouse.

Jumpstart Your Happiness

If it is to be, it is up to me

By Kellie Poulsen-Grill

It was 10 a.m. on Tuesday on a beautiful Springtime morning in Wilsonville, Oregon. All of our 11 horses had been fed, and I had an English muffin toasted and ready to eat for breakfast. I took it, along with my steaming hot cup of tea in my favorite ceramic horse mug, and walked into my home office. I sat down at my computer and, taking a bite of the muffin and a sip of my tea, I reached over to shake my computer mouse and clicked on the tab to open my emails.

To my surprise, there was an email from another horse woman and horse-lover like me, my dear friend Debbi. I could see that it had been sent in a group to 14 ladies, a few of whose names I recognized, as they were other horse women whom Debbi knew from the horse boarding barn when she lived here in Oregon a few years ago. They were Debbi's "horse buddies," and I was one of Debbi's horse buddies, too.

Ever since Tom, Debbi's husband, transferred to Albuquerque for his job 3 years ago, Debbi always called me on the phone to check in and catch up, so it was rare to see an email from her. Tears started to stream down my face as I saw the words Debbi had typed: *I'm so sorry to tell you this in an email, but I wanted to let you all know, and this is the best way I could think of to do that. It is with great sadness that I tell you all, I have a form of very aggressive breast cancer, and the rest of this remaining year will be filled with a double mastectomy, radiation, chemotherapy, and then reconstructive surgery. I went to my annual mammogram appointment and they found a lump in my left breast. It was cancer, and they are acting as fast as they can to save my life. If I hadn't gone to my mammogram appointment, they think I would have died within months. I'm going to fight like crazy to win this battle, however, the doctors say it will be a very tough war. I'm writing to ask for your prayers, lots of them, and a favor... We all are horse women. We all know the healing power of horses. I am asking for you all to go to your horses for me. Please lay your hands on each and every one of them, and ask them to help heal me. Ask them to give me their magical strength to be brave as I fight this awful battle. I need you all to pray, and I need your horses, along with God, to help heal me and let me live. I love you all, Debbi.*

I was a blubbering, crying mess when I finished reading, and I hit reply on the email. I answered back, my hands shaking as I typed, tears dripping onto my keyboard. My chest was heaving, and I almost couldn't type. I replied *Absolutely, I will do that, and I will be praying so very hard for you to heal and to get through all of your surgeries and your chemo and radiation treatments. I am going right now out to the pasture to lay my hands on all 11 of our horses, to ask them to heal, comfort, and give their strength to you, my amazing, beautiful friend whom I dearly love.*

Debbi fought a hard and tough battle for over a year with her breast cancer and surgeries. I went to visit her twice to give her comfort and to make her smile. Back in Oregon at my home and horse ranch, I'd go out to our horses and ask for their strength and healing powers for Debbi. After a hard-fought battle, I'm thrilled to say that Debbi has made a full recovery! She is alive, and a 7-year breast cancer survivor!

I'm sharing Debbi's story with you because I think there are great lessons in happiness to be learned from it. When I got the news about Debbi, I became a hysterical, crying mess. I was sad. I was broken-hearted and I was spiraling down into darkness. Those who know me know that I am ALWAYS happy. People meet me and they say, "Oh my gosh I just LOVE your energy! Are you always this upbeat and happy and kind?" And Dave, my husband, will say, "Yep—that's Kellie!"

I am a happy person who has taken anything negative that has happened to me in my 54 years of living (and believe me, there have been plenty of obstacles and challenges in my life), and I've decided to make the best of it. I've decided to CHOOSE HAPPINESS, no matter what. We can either dwell in sadness and pain, or we can choose to rise above it and do better. I've heard that we don't find a happy life; we make it. We have to realize that no one is going to rescue us; we have to rescue ourselves, and find our own joy. We must decide to live lives full of happiness.

When Debbi was diagnosed with breast cancer, it shook me to my core. My husband Dave's first wife, Teresa, had died of breast cancer at 40 years old, leaving him and his 3 children behind. Thankfully, Dave and the kids and I were able to become a family, and I was able to step in as a wife and stepmom--but obviously breast cancer is a very sensitive subject for our family.

After I replied to Debbie's email, I called Dave on my cell phone as I was pulling on my boots to go be with the horses. I told him the news about Debbi. I was crying hard, and having such a difficult time with this news. He left work and found me in the pasture, loving on, hugging on, and crying on the horses. He said to them, "Our Kellie is sad." I cried in his arms and took deep breaths. The horses gathered around us, giving us their strength, magical healing, and love.

Throughout that day, I laid around on the couch and in bed. It felt almost like I had the flu. Everything hurt, and my heart felt broken. Dave got me chicken noodle soup and he tried his best to comfort and calm me. I was feeling extremely down, and felt very afraid that my friend Debbi would die.

Then it hit me: I had been professionally speaking about happiness for over 5 years, I had written 3 books on happiness, I was a happiness expert--and I was not practicing anything that I had taught or spoken about. I was being a victim. I was acting helpless. I was letting negativity overtake me. There is an old saying: "Be better, not bitter." I was so mad at cancer! I was wallowing in self-pity, hurt, and fear. Nothing I was currently doing or feeling was going to help Debbi. All it was doing was hurting me. It was going to take me down, and if I wasn't careful, I might allow this turn of events to destroy my happy, awesome life.

I got up out of bed. I got showered, I got dressed, I put on makeup and styled my hair. I put on my favorite music and started singing. I started to make dinner. Our three children would be home from school soon, and I was not going to bring them down. I'd tell them about Debbi; they all knew her and loved her, too. I would probably cry as I told them, but I would show them strength. I would show them hope for her recovery, and I would show them that we are only as happy as we make up our minds to be. Happiness is something we must work on: like our muscles, happiness is something we must build to strengthen. A positive attitude creates a positive and happy life.

Life is hard. It is full of obstacles and challenges. If life wasn't full of these things, well then, it wouldn't be life.

How we react to things that happen to us will determine our destiny. Do you want a happy life? If you do, then remember this saying: "If it is to be, it is up to me."

I wish you HUGE HAPPINESS and JOY in your life. You deserve it. It is your birthright. Stay grateful, stay positive, and stay focused on happiness. You were destined to be happy. Consciously choose happiness every day, and happiness will be yours.

If you'd like my FREE Download, *Kellie Poulsen-Grill's 7 Strategies for Staying Happy,* just go to www.HappinessAndJoyRetreats.com/jumpstart and pick it up!

About the Author
Kellie Poulsen-Grill

Kellie Poulsen-Grill is a certified Equine Gestalt Coach, Happiness Expert, Professional Speaker & Songwriter, Best-Selling Author, Publisher, and Send Out Cards affiliate. She owns Happy Success Ranch Retreats, where she hosts retreats with her horses in Wilsonville, OR. Kellie is married to Dave Grill. They have 3 children and 6 grandchildren. They have 30 "fur babies," 12 horses, 2 pet steers, 3 dogs, 9 cats, and 4 ducks.

Jumpstart Your Health

Improve Your Gut and Improve Your Health

By Joan Lorrain

I was six years old, running along the water, on the San Francisco beach. The waves ebbed back and forth, splashing and speeding towards my bare feet. I ran alongside the foaming blue-green water. I was just to the left of the pair of large, bright-red tennis shoes, watching them kicking up chunks of wet sand. I was running along the beach with my daddy. I was careful to follow closely, as I jumped from one seaweed patch to the next. I have many fond memories of both of my parents demonstrating the importance of healthy routines.

From an early age, I watched my father follow an exercise regimen. Sometimes, I would even sit on his feet as he did his sit-ups, helping him count: one, two, three. . .

My mom was a nurse. She was totally focused on teaching us about eating nutritious foods. I already knew that I enjoyed the way I felt when I ate lots of vegetables, and could not help but notice how low-energy I felt when I ate something like a hot dog. Mom became diabetic around 45 years old, which caused her to become especially focused on teaching us about proper nutrition. Diabetes ran on her side of the family.

Everyone is biologically different. Some of us are predisposed to certain diseases. We can choose not to turn on the disease gene marker, by avoiding the trigger foods and toxins that can turn these "disease genes" on.

We must educate ourselves, listen to our bodies, and be our own best health advocates. We must be patient with ourselves, as we discover what our bodies need from us in order to flourish.

I always knew I might get diabetes one day. I wasn't perfect, but I wasn't that off track, either, with my healthy routines. I even gave up cake decorating to minimize my time spent around cake!

To my dismay, a few years back, I became pre-diabetic. The doctor sent me to a diabetic class. I increased my exercising, and I ate more cautiously. Eleven short months later, I got the call. I was diabetic. I was shocked!

I had read many books on diabetes, and I knew other people had gotten in many more years before becoming diabetic. I felt cheated. Things just got worse from there, despite all of my increased efforts.

Eventually, I was able to reverse my diabetes. It wasn't easy, but I did it.

My studies at the Institute of Integrative Nutrition (IIN) taught me that it is important to treat the whole person. I discovered that Naturopathic Doctors and Functional Medicine Doctors are well-versed in treating root causes, and these professionals have attracted many western doctors to move over to these rewarding fields.

Understanding what makes us thrive, as a Life and Integrative Nutrition Coach, I have had the joy of helping so many others to jumpstart their health, to realize their dreams.

It is valuable to work with both your doctor and other professionals to address the root causes of disease.

You might want to do what I did. I found a Functional Medicine doctor, who was also an M.D., to work with me regarding my health concerns.

Here are the 7 Tips to Jumpstart your Health.

You might want to keep a daily food/water log, and note how you are feeling each day as you jumpstart your health.

Tip #1: Improve Gut Health – by taking probiotics and possibly prebiotics.

You may have heard the quote by Hippocrates, "All diseases begin in the gut."

To improve your gut health, you will want to reduce leaky gut and repair your gut lining. You will absorb more nutrients.

We have good and bad bacteria in our gut. This is our gut flora. By eating fermented foods daily, we are replacing beneficial bacteria. Raw Apple Cider, pickled vegetables, and fermented foods such as Kefir, sauerkraut, Kombucha, kimchi, and fermented soy, called tempeh, are all great options.

Eat meals without water/drink. Water dilutes stomach acid. Eat more real, organic, whole foods, and healthy fats. Eat the rainbow when it comes to eating both fruits and vegetables. Be sure to eat avocados, coconut, and dark leafy greens. Eat berries, high in fiber and antioxidants, and select options that are low in sugar. Eat hormone-free, grass-fed meat, wild salmon, and sardines.

Photo of Hippocrates statue taken by Raed Mansour. "All diseases begin in the gut." ~ Hippocrates

Tip #2: Improve Gut Lining, by drinking bone broth.

Drink grass-fed beef broth, free-range chicken broth, or fish head broth every day. Bone broth heals the mucosal lining of the gut. It reduces inflammation, improves immunity, benefits sleep, benefits skin, hair, bones, and arteries, and it contains glycosaminoglycans to protect our joints.

Tip #3: Drink 8 cups of clean filtered water or more, daily.

Drinking water after meals keeps us hydrated, detoxes us, and helps digestion. I like to start the day with either a cup of hot water with a tablespoon of raw apple cider, or lemon juice. This starts up my metabolism and burns fat.

Tip #4: Move as much as you can, every day.

High Intensity Intermediate Training (HIIT) Exercise is essential for good health. It minimizes stress, reduces inflammation, builds muscle, strengthens our heart, detoxes our body, creates more energy and mental clarity. Check in with your doctor prior to doing any exercise program. Exercise should be what you enjoy, so you're more likely to do it. Be sure it includes a form of aerobics, weights, and stretching.

You might want to try the following HIIT exercise. You can do this on the treadmill, or on a stationary bike. Start out by running fast, or peddling very fast, for two minutes. Then go slow for four minutes, fast for two minutes, and again, slow for four minutes, maintaining this pattern until you reach 30 minutes.

HIIT exercise should be done once a week. It targets the visceral fat around your belly and melts it away. Allow for the muscles to rest for a couple of days after doing a HIIT exercise. The toxins seep from the visceral fat, and then clear away. If you do not skip a few days, the toxins can build up in the liver. (See the study on JoanLorrain.com.)

Tip #5: Sleep. Always get 8 to 9 hours every day.

When we sleep, we detox, heal, and repair our bodies. If we don't get enough sleep, we develop low-grade inflammation, brain fog, and increased hunger. Inflammation left unchecked becomes chronic disease, i.e. heart disease, high cholesterol, diabetes, and others.

Tip #6: Minimize toxin intake and/or exposure, to the best of your ability.

Every day, we are surrounded with environmental toxins: in our air, our food, and our water. Pesticides, GMOs, and other chemicals are in our conventional foods and water.

If possible, limit white foods like sugar, white flour, and white rice. Minimize eating boxed or packaged foods. Many of us are intolerant to sugar, gluten, and processed foods, causing allergies and autoimmune responses. Plan to cook simple, healthy meals often.

Every time we minimize toxins, increase our water, or get adequate sleep, and we increase our daily movement, we begin to see and feel the healing process. It feels very empowering!

Tip #7: Work with a health or wellness coach.

At the renowned Mayo Clinic, an American nonprofit academic medical center, there was a study with 100 participants who worked with a health coach. They found that the majority of these people improved their health. They were able to lose weight, create healthy habits, and increase physical activity by participating in a 12-week program. The University of San Francisco had a similar study, with similar results. This study describes how health coaches and patients worked together. The study highlighted factors such as availability, trust, education, personal support, and decision-making support. Working with the health coaches bridged the gap between the patient and the clinician.

Read everything you can on the topic of health. When it comes to the scientific evidence, make sure the scientific study is conducted by a third party, and not by the source making the claim. Two great, free research sources are WebMd and PubMed.

If you have had difficulty doing the things you know you need to do, partner with a health coach. You will discover creative ways to reduce stress, find clarity, and finally, manifest your good health and reach many other longed-for goals.

Tip #8 (BONUS): Manage stress daily to reverse signs of aging, eliminate toxins, and reduce disease. I do a daily ten-minute meditation to manage my stress and rejuvenate. To get you started right now on reducing your stress, **I want to give you my meditation video for FREE! I also created a quick, easy recipe book that you can sign up for, plus many more free gifts, and resources to help you reduce stress and jumpstart your health. Just go to www.JoanLorrain.com/jumpstart today!**

You're also welcome to contact me if you have questions or concerns; I would love to meet you and see how we can partner together to find the answers you are seeking.

About the Author
Joan Lorrain

Joan is an Integrative Health and Life Coach who appreciates the benefits of whole foods and holistic living. She studied at the Institute of Integrative Nutrition (IIN) and has completed additional years of her own extensive studies on the progression of many chronic diseases and autoimmune diseases present in our society today. It has sparked an interest in learning more about the toxins in our water, food, household cleaning, and personal hygiene products.

Jumpstart Your Love Life

Getting What You Want Because You Deserve It

By Katrina Sawa

This chapter is for all of you who are either in a relationship now, or who want to be in one. It's written from the perspective of being an entrepreneur, and the unique struggles we go through in having to find (or mold) the perfect partner.

But before we *find* the perfect partner--or even *evaluate* our current significant-other-relationships--we must evaluate our own level of self-love. Love for ourselves is the first thing we have to get comfortable with. I don't think there is anyone I've ever met, entrepreneur or not, who doesn't feel some level of discomfort with him- or herself.

Do you truly love yourself?

Do you believe that you deserve the most amazing partner in your life?

Are you currently *being* that amazing partner whom *they* deserve?

If not, it could be time for a little self-reflection.

So, why is a Business and Marketing Coach writing about Jumpstarting Your Love Life? Well, because I've done some firsthand work in this area of my life, and I've developed some useful systems, just like in business, for dating and relationship communication. I also wrote a book called *Love Yourself Successful* that helps people identify what they truly want and gives them the confidence to go after it.

If you're not satisfied with where you are right now in your love life, then why not see if my advice can help you. If you *think you're good* right now in your love life, I encourage you to make sure you're not settling. I've seen this over and over again with my clients when we really dive into what's going on with them in their personal lives. Together, we've been able to identify and resolve problems whose solutions have led to a tremendous increase in the level of happiness. So, read this with an open heart.

One thing **I'm REALLY GOOD AT is** helping you communicate your needs, visions, passions, and purpose with your loved ones so they can begin to really understand you and what you need from them I can also help you to communicate better in general, and to better manage your energy when you're around them.

This all stemmed from when I analyzed my relationship with my first husband after I became

an entrepreneur. I learned that he no longer "got me." After being married six and a half years, he became fearful that I wouldn't bring in a steady paycheck anymore. He would say things to me, little digs, that hurt very much and didn't encourage me at all. In fact, I would go out to networking events during the day with a big smile on my face, tell everyone that everything was ok, and then cry myself to sleep because I felt like I wasn't loved or supported. I spent two years like that, trying to make him understand my new goals. He didn't have any interest in knowing what it was that I did, or in understanding me.

I don't want you to be in a situation like this. It hurts not to be supported in what you really want to do or be. I wasn't willing to settle any longer, and I hope you aren't either. I was 35 years old at the time. I asked myself, "Do I want to live like this for the next 40-50 years?"

Do you feel like you keep reliving the same relationships with different people over and over, and can't figure out why?

If you're finally ready to break the cycle of unfulfilling or drama-filled relationships, and meet an amazing partner within the next year, you will want to do some things differently.

Perhaps it could be time for you to:

- Clear out the love blockages that are keeping you stuck in the same relationship patterns.

- Learn how to prepare yourself to welcome the love of your life.

- Take the necessary steps to attracting this special person.

- Maintain a lasting, fulfilling relationship, and continue creating the initial chemistry you experienced in the beginning.

Whether you are unhappy being single, unhappy in your marriage or relationship, or simply feel like you need a few improvements, I want you to realize that you don't have to settle. The grass CAN be greener if you are willing to put yourself out there and take a stand for what you really want.

Here are the first six of the 53 things I had on my "Want/Need List" when I was looking for my current husband in 2012:

1. Highly motivated in business, but still believes in having balance, goals, and ambition.

2. Would put me first and/or think of me all the time (at the store, with friends, in the car, when with his kids etc.).

3. Very affectionate and attentive (in public and private).

4. Outgoing and sociable when the occasion called for it (since that's a big part of my life and business).

5. Somewhat interested in being a homebody, at least part-time: home improvements, gardening, sitting around on the weekends watching movies, or entertaining.

6. Somewhat romantic, if not downright romantic and thoughtful (e.g. sends flowers, gives cards, leaves notes, cooks dinner, etc.).

I'll give you the whole list on my website so you can see how detailed I was when I was looking for my Mr. Right. I read these every day like a mantra, similar to how some people say their affirmations. This can also work with your current relationship, if you make this list to see whether your current partner fits the majority of them and, if not, what gradual adjustments can be made. My husband, Jason, fit 95% of these.

I hate to see anyone being unhappy in their love life. Frankly, having an amazing husband like I do now is one of the single best things that I have going for me. It allows me to be more confident in what I'm doing, and it allows me to be proud and bold with the decisions that I make in order to grow my business every year.

I remember when I was single and dating, and I longed for a loving relationship like this. It was on my mind pretty much every day, which affected my ability to really work my business the way it needed to be worked. I wasn't as motivated, I wasn't as confident, and I wasn't taking the action steps that I needed to take on a regular basis because I wasn't fully happy.

I believe to the core of my being that when we love ourselves, and when others around us fully love and support us, that is when we will be able to pour our best selves into our families, our clients, and to the world.

Back in 2012 I was so serious about finding my Mr. Right that I hired a $6,000 matchmaking service, and I was actively searching for my man on four online dating sites as well (some paid and some free). I even invested another $3,500 and attended three relationship-oriented workshops in person to help me discover what I really wanted for myself, in a relationship/partnership, in a man, etc.

With $10,000 invested in my search for my Mr. Right, I was "all in," as they say, and doing everything I could possibly do. **(I found him 6 months into my search that year!)**

I grew so much during that time. I learned what I had been doing WRONG with men in the last forty-something years, and how I could change it moving forward.

During that time online, I had to develop systems for reaching out to and connecting with potential men, because I knew it would be like finding a needle in a haystack and I wanted to meet 100 men to find my Mr. Right. I decided to focus about 20-30% of my time on this endeavor, and I knew that in order to reach that many men quickly, I would have to develop systems.

I had to really shift my mindset, because I couldn't let myself get too attached to any one man too early on or else I wouldn't reach enough men. It's a numbers game, just like in business/marketing. I call it *sorting*, not dating.

Now, Jason and I are married and happier than either of us had ever imagined! I want everyone to be as happy and successful as I am, and I'm not going to stop sharing my message until that happens.

It's time to finally take charge of your life and design the business of your dreams!

I have a few programs that can help you either to love yourself more and/or to find your Mr./Mrs. Right. I've put information about these programs on the same page as some free gifts I want to share!

Go to www.JumpstartYourLoveLife.net and you'll get access to all of it:

- My Mr. Right List of 53 Things

- 2 Free Interviews with Tips on Online Dating Success

- Relationship Needs Worksheet - Good to Evaluate Your Current Relationship or New

Here's hoping you find and enjoy a lot more love in your life! *YOU DESERVE IT!*

About the Author
Katrina Sawa

Katrina Sawa is an award-winning international speaker and business coach who kicks her clients and their businesses into high gear! She is the author of 11 books including *Love Yourself Successful*, and she's the creator of the Love Yourself Successful Teleseries and Online Dating Program for Women Over 40. She loves to inspire and educate other entrepreneurs on how to get more love in their life and money in their business.

Jumpstart Your Nutrition

Nutrition Tips You Don't Get from Your Regular Doctor

By Yvonne M. Rea

Hippocrates, the Greek founder of western medicine, considered nutrition to be one of the main tools that a doctor can use to restore and maintain health.

Have you ever been at a health food store, standing in the vitamin aisle, looking at the vast sea of different boxes and bottles thinking, "Where do I start??" Not only are YOU confused, but practically everyone else in the aisle is also scratching their head and asking questions like: "Which ones are *really* going to work for me? Do I *really* need all of these?" Or maybe the thought is, "I eat right and exercise. I'm on a good nutritional regime. What's the bare minimum *I* need to take?"

Well, you must first understand that our food alone is no longer enough to keep us healthy. Data shows that we can no longer get all the key nutrients from our food. That's because our soil is depleted of minerals. If there are no minerals in the soil, then they're not in the plants. If there are no minerals in the plants, the people eating plants without supplementing will have mineral deficiency conditions. In addition to that, upwards of 80% of the supplements on the shelves, and through the internet, are synthetic (made in a petri dish, in a laboratory). So, unlike food, it's **NOT REAL**; it's an isolate, and not full-spectrum. Plus, it's only partially absorbable. As of the early 1980's, there is a known standard: the minimum number of nutrients to keep the body from breaking down. There are 90 nutrients that are considered key to promoting life, aiding in weight loss, detoxing the system of toxins and free radicals, and repairing tissue break down from deficiency.

If you're that person in the vitamin aisle, then I want to share with you the 5 Key Proven Steps to Jumpstart your Nutritional Regime, and help you improve your overall health and weight. For a better you, I will make you aware of things that most of us did not know, things that go against the grain. This is not community college-level information, this is elite college-level information with a system and methods reserved for the elite and wealthy.

If you're a health advocate and have knowledge about vitamins and minerals but don't have a proven system for relating them to disease, then implementing these 5 key steps will be the start of measurable health results and you will consistently have more wildly happy customers!

As a former military medic, I worked in surgical wards, assisted in autopsies, and I even ran dental departments in two of the largest military hospitals. My military career was vast, expanding from Medical Clinics, to Ship, to the Navy Ski Team. It was here where my love for the sciences began.

While serving with the Marines, I, along with over a million others, were hit with "friendly fire" via chemical exposure. My health quickly began to deteriorate. Yet, all the doctors, pills, and endless therapies did not help me. In fact, they made me worse.

Being military, I like following systems and researching. So, in 2008, I began looking elsewhere, outside of the medical community and far onto the horizon. What has taken me thousands of hours of school, internships, research, and volunteer work experience, not to mention thousands of dollars and my own personal trials--I am now sharing with you.

During those years of research, I learned that the true root cause of death, disease, and discomfort is inadequate nutrition. To me, documentation beats conversation every time. With this discovery and the education and training I received, I began to gain back my health. I'm still working on greater healing. It takes time, but I am no longer facing imminent death or feeling down for weeks at a time because of pain and lack of energy.

My purpose here is twofold:

1. To show you the research and data about THEKEY90. THEKEY90 Nutrients is the largest known study ever done on nutrition as it relates to disease in the body. This is the system that I've

followed and continue to teach my clients, and it works!

2. To show you the truth about nutrition and disease in general. Even the National Institute of Health Science and the CDC say 7 out of 10 deaths are due to inadequate nutrition. The health community wants us to think it takes 14 years of schooling and a degree to understand this system for optimal health. Well, grab your notepad and Let's go Play Doctor!

Nutritional diseases are known, and very common. Most are only treated with pharmaceuticals. Research is clear: severe Vitamin A deficiencies in children cause keratitis, corneal ulcers, and blindness. Calcium (4th most used nutrient in the body) deficiency contributes to osteoporosis, arthritis, blood pressure issues, panic attacks, and more. Iodine and copper deficiencies cause goiter in adults, and miscarriages. Infants with spina bifida and serious cleft palates are a result of folic acid and zinc deficiencies. EFA's can lower Serum cholesterol and alleviate menopause symptoms, all while increasing brain function--plus they can help your hubby with sexual stamina.

The most significant (and overlooked) health discovery of the 21st Century was from the Mutual of Omaha, along with The National Institute of Health & Science. This was a 12-½-year study on Nutrition & Disease in the Body. This was the largest study, consisting of 25,000 autopsies and 10 million blood smears. This study identified the key 90 nutrients, and is so highly regarded that it is housed in The Smithsonian. What started with animals has extended to humans, proving the elimination of hundreds of degenerative diseases and doubling lifespans.

The research showed that these Key 90 Nutrients are essential nutrients, necessary for life. The "Key" or "Essential Nutrients" designation means each nutrient on the list is a nutrient that must be taken into the body via supplementation because the body doesn't make it, and without it, the body cannot completely live or repair. They're necessary for the body to stave off illness, facilitate repair, and, if given in the right dose, allow your body to *thrive!*

The Key 90 minerals and nutrients found during this 12 ½-year study on Nutrition and Disease in the Body, include:

- 60 minerals

- 16 vitamins

- 12 amino acids

- 3 Essential fatty acids/Omegas

Note 2/3 of the Key 90 nutrients are minerals. Vitamins without minerals are useless. Vitamins are not complete without the cofactor minerals. These cofactors help the body to better absorb the vitamins and get them into the various body systems. When you feed your body the proper nutrition it needs on a daily basis, you begin to reverse and repair the micro-tears and rebuild the body.

Here is the overview of the 5-Step KEY 90 Protocol. Do this, and you will quickly learn which of these raw nutrients will help you to overcome or avoid the health challenges, issues, and diseases.

1. Identify the Health Category using the Self Evaluation - I have a tool for this to which you can obtain free access at the end of this chapter!

2. Consume Enough of THEKEY90 Nutrients, of which I will give you a list as well...but here are 3 Main Concepts for when you're standing in the vitamin aisle now:

   • Select only whole food-based powders, supplements, or liquids. Do not select synthetic options.

   • Your selection must include all of The Key 90 Nutrients. Very few companies offer an all-in-one multivitamin with The Key 90 Nutrients, so bear in mind, you may be purchasing several boxes and bottles to add up to The Key 90 Nutrients.

   • Powder to liquid form is most bioavailable. This means it is better absorbed into the body than pill form. Most people do not have good gut health to begin with, and so breaking down pills and absorbing the minerals and nutrients is more difficult for most peoples' systems to handle. Plus, 8 out of 10 people take some kind of prescribed medication, which also blocks the body's ability to absorb.

3. Eliminate toxic, inflammatory, and carcinogenic foods, such as wheat, rye, barley, and oats, as well as charred meats, baked potatoes, and processed meats. There are more, and I also have a list for this!

4. PDCA = Plan-Do-Check-Adjust every 30 days for 90-120 days.

5. Keep notes and get out of the way.

For many, this endeavor will cost you more than you're used to spending on your health, but it will be worth it. As your health and strength grow, your fuel/energy levels will increase as well. Most of us have never had all 90 nutrients, because most multivitamins only contain 32 nutrients.

I and over 2,100 others I've helped, are living proof that through these natural methods we have been able to lose weight, repair our health and the damage done to our bodies, when traditional methods could not. 80+% feel a significant difference within 30 days. With this proven research and expert help, I have taken THEKEY90 and designed a simple Health Map and the 4 Health Categories to shorten your learning curve.

I want to gift you access to some of these initial materials and lists so that you can get started today!

When you go to my site, you'll receive the rest of the THEKEY90+ Protocols, which include THEKEY90 Nutrients, The Health Map, the Good Food, Bad Food List, and the 4 Health Categories Self-Evaluation List. Go to www.JumpstartYourNutritionNow.com today!

About the Author
Yvonne M. Rea

During her Military service, Yvonne found a love for the sciences after assisting in numerous forensic identification cases, and has logged in thousands of school and research hours covering nutritional science as it relates to disease. Some recent Studies & Certifications include Bioelectro-physiology, Nutrition, Functional Medicine, and she is owner of 4ABETTERU2 Wellness Resources: Making the Unknown Known, where "85% notice a significant difference." Yvonne currently works with Health Centers, Health Coaches, Advocates, and those patients who are looking for a second chance at better health.

Jumpstart Your Parenting Skills

3 Tips for Creating a Stronger Relationship with Your Child

By Samantha Foote

Do you wonder what your child is trying to communicate through their behavior?

Do you wonder how to stop nagging and punishing in order to help your child engage in positive behavior?

Are you living in chaos and frustration?

This chapter is intended to help you enhance your relationship with your child and give you a starting point to begin the process of improving communication with your child by using positive parenting strategies.

The 3 tips I'm giving here are great for parenting a child at any age, and they are the foundation for positive parenting.

My 3 Top Tips for Positive Parenting

1. Understand what your child is *REALLY* communicating

Behavior is communication. Your child doesn't do something just to do it. There is a reason why they are doing what they are doing. One reason your child may be acting out is because they want attention (good or bad).

If your child is misbehaving to get your attention, here are some things you can do:

- Give them a larger amount of attention when they do something well, or when they ask for your attention appropriately.

- Over-give attention to the good things. Give attention immediately, and then back off, making them wait for a certain amount of time.

- Ignore the negative behavior as much as possible.

Another reason your child may act out is because they can't have something they want, or they can't do what they want.

Do your kids ever get frustrated and yell, scream, or stomp their feet when you tell them "no" to something they want? Do they continue to argue as to why they should get what they want?

If this is the cause of your child misbehaving, you can give them options of things they can have or do.

For example, my son asked to watch a movie the other day, but the answer was "no." He cried and argued for a bit, but then I gave him options of other things that he could do. He picked one, and went on to do that activity.

If your child is misbehaving because they can't have or do something they want, here are a few things you can try:

- Ask why they think they can't have it.

- Give choices of what they can do.

- If they argue, tell them why they can't have something, and leave it at that. You can say you are going to ignore them if they keep arguing.

A third reason that your child may act out is that, when you tell them or ask them to do something you need them to do, they don't want to do it.

Have you ever asked your child to do something, such as turn the TV off, put down their electronic device, do the dishes, etc. and they reacted poorly? They may have run away, stomped, screamed, etc.

If your child is misbehaving because they don't want to do something they have been asked to do, here are a few things you can try:

- Set up routines and schedules so they know what is expected.

- Write down your schedule for the whole day in a way that your child can see it and understand what comes next in their day.

- Set consequences if they don't do it. Ask for their opinion on what these consequences should be. Remember, they can offer an opinion on the consequence, but you have the power to make the final decision.

For Example: If your child has a hard time going to bed at night, making an evening routine can be extremely helpful. You can make a 'picture schedule' or 'written schedule' on paper, or you can download an app and use that. I like to use the app "Visual Schedules and Social Stories." In this app, you can create multiple different schedules such as morning routines, evening routines, cleaning your room, etc. The evening routine may include picking up their room, getting things ready for the next day, putting on pajamas, brushing teeth, reading, and then going to bed. Schedules can also be found online. If you Google "Evening routine schedule" or "Bedtime routine schedule," multiple schedules will pop up.

Finally, another reason that your kids may act out that we, as parents, hardly ever think about, is that they have uncomfortable feelings about their body and they may not understand why.

Sometimes, kids' bodies just don't feel right, and they don't know how to express their feelings about it, or they don't know exactly what's wrong or how to fix it.

For example: My son says that most of his clothes are uncomfortable and make him itchy. To fix this, I cut the tags out of the clothes that were bugging him. He also doesn't like wearing long-sleeved shirts, so we roll his sleeves or just buy short-sleeved shirts. His clothing discomfort was not something that he just came out and expressed to me the first time it happened. He cried and screamed every time he was asked to put a shirt on that was uncomfortable.

It took some time before we were able to figure out what was bothering him.

The way you can tell if it's a sensory issue versus just a tantrum, is what happens when you remove the thing that's bothering them, or you give them the sensory input they need. If the misbehavior stops immediately after fixing what is bothering them, then it is a sensory issue. If they continue to misbehave, there is something else causing the behavior.

2. **Control your reactions and plan your strategy**

After you figure out why your child is doing what they are doing, think of what will benefit your child in the long run before you react.

Sometimes our instant reactions can be automatically negative, like being frustrated or angry, and that's normal. However, consider attempting to pause first to determine what is best for your child. Is it important for you to just punish your child for their behavior, or is there a way you can have them learn from the experience and discover what they can do better next time?

For Example: My 3-year-old often gets very overwhelmed with life. He will scream, cry, or hit when he is frustrated. When he does this, my first instinct is to put him in the corner and tell him he's in time-out.

There's something else I can do though. Instead of just punishing him, I can use a positive strategy to teach him how to manage his frustration and calm himself down before he gets to the point of screaming, crying, or hitting.

A positive strategy that I use in this situation is when I notice he is getting frustrated, I get down on his level and ask him if he would like to take a break and take deep breaths. Sometimes he says yes, and sometimes he says no. If he says no, I tell him that I need to take deep breaths and invite him to join me. He will then take deep breaths with me, or at least sit quietly while I take deep breaths. He is still learning how to calm himself, but sometimes he will come and get me when he is frustrated, and ask to take deep breaths with me.

3. **Be Consistent in everything you do.**

No matter what strategy you choose, be consistent. Say what you mean, and follow through. Don't make threats with which you can't follow through. Kids aren't dumb. They know when you are making an empty threat and when you will actually follow through. Just remember that it will generally get worse before it gets better. Kids often do something for the reaction that they want. If it doesn't get them what they want, they may try it more just to see if they get the same result. Eventually, they will stop doing that behavior because it's not getting them what they want.

For example: When my son was younger and wanted candy, he would ask for candy. If he couldn't have it, I told him "Not right now." He would then cry and yell for several minutes. If I would have given in and given him candy, he would have learned that his crying and yelling got him what he wanted. I stayed consistent though, and now he is still disappointed when I tell him "no," but he does not argue, cry, or yell.

I would love to invite you to share your feedback as you try out these positive parenting techniques.

- Did you implement a technique?

- How did it work for you?

- Do you need additional support?

My website has helpful parenting information and programs that you can check out. **I've even created a special page just for you where I included a FREE Webinar on the topic of these 3 Tips where I go into much more depth. If you'd like to listen to that, then go to www.BoiseMusicTherapyCompany. com/jumpstart.**

You will also get a FREE Membership in my strategy-of-the-month club for more ideas about how to use positive parenting strategies, plus some discounts on my programs too!

About the Author

Samantha Foote

Samantha is a neurologic, board-certified Music Therapist, a Certified Habilitative Intervention Professional, and a registered Positive Discipline Parent Educator. She has been working with parents and children for 15 years and has 3 children of her own. Samantha's mission is to help parents and children develop deeper relationships through the use of positive parenting strategies. When she is not working, Samantha enjoys camping and other outdoor adventures with her family.

Jumpstart Your Pet Relationship

Building a Stronger Bond with Your Pet

By Gillian H. Edwards

Do you ever wonder what your pet is thinking or feeling? Have you ever experienced a moment when you thought your pet was trying to send you a message? Ever wondered why they might be acting a certain way, or even reacting differently to a new situation? Most of the time, even if you're not aware of it, they are trying to communicate with you. Just like humans, animals have thoughts and feelings. So how can you better understand what they are trying to say? How can you understand their deepest desires? You can either pretend you know, or make up what your pet is saying...or you can work with an animal communicator, like myself!

What's an animal communicator?

Animal communicators are individuals who possess a unique ability to "talk" with animals: hearing, seeing, and understanding their thoughts and feelings, and deeply tuning in to what an animal is trying to express.

"Oh, come on, that doesn't work," is what I often hear from skeptics at this point. But hang in here with me for a moment, and maybe I can enlighten you.

How does animal communication work?

Sometimes referred to as a "sixth sense," animal communication involves the direct transmission of feelings, emotions, thoughts, mental images, and more, to connect telepathically. This means mentally sending and receiving messages to and from your pets, sometimes without using sensory channels like sound, or physical interaction. Animals are masters of telepathic communication. They speak to each other in this manner, and they also attempt to speak to humans in the same way.

How do I know you are communicating with my Bella?

Think of it as a wireless IP address. You want to print a document from your computer. Your computer contacts your router to look for your printer, and it prints to the one with which it is connected. Put another way, it's like radio waves. If you want to listen to pop/adult contemporary music on the radio, you turn the dial and tune to that station, and when you do, you don't expect to hear jazz or the blues. When connecting with your animal remotely, a picture and a name is the equivalent of the IP address or radio wave. Even when they have crossed over, it is still possible to connect to their energy wave.

How did this world come to me?

How did I know I could communicate with animals? As an intuitive healer, I have worked with energies for a number of years and I was with a human patient when I 'heard' a voice. Looking around, I noticed the pet dog in the corner watching me, and didn't think much of it. So, I went back to focusing on my patient, when I heard the voice again. Now the dog and I were staring at each other in earnest. Was I crazy? Had I imagined it, or was it real? I Googled it when I got home that night. It was real. I found teachers to help me on this new path of understanding, and began a journey filled with wonder. I went from observing to understanding that every animal is an individual with their own personalities and sense of humor. Then I realized the animals are really the teachers, with whom I share a deep love and respect, and from whom I continue to learn. All species, domestic or wild, have a voice to be heard, a story to tell. It doesn't matter whether it's a horse, a cat, a rabbit, a whale, an eagle, or a squirrel. It doesn't matter whether you call me an animal communicator, whisperer, intuitive, or psychic. My work with animals reinforces our connection, our cohabitation, and our understanding of animal cognition and behavior.

So how can animal communication benefit you and your pet?

First, it can be used to enrich relationships and bonds between animals and their owners. It can also be used as a form of distance or in-person healing, and can be applied to many situations, including health problems, general check-ins, improving behavioral issues, aging, end-of-life decisions...it can help you to make the best decisions for you and your pets, and much more.

Often, pet parents will reach out to me to figure out what is going on with their animals, and to help them make decisions regarding their pets. While some just want to check in and make sure everything is going well, others have specific reasons why they want to better understand what their pet is trying to tell them.

Maybe a pet just had, or needs, surgery, or there's a sudden change in behavior. Or, a beloved pet is nearing the end of its life, and the parent isn't exactly sure how to say goodbye. Or, the pet has crossed the rainbow bridge, and the parent has one more message of love for them. Other common reasons why pet parents reach out to me are: to understand why there is friction when a new pet is introduced into the household and what to do about it, to find out whether a pet likes its vet, whether it likes its trainer, or even whether it enjoys its food!

Remember, just like humans, animals have thoughts and feelings. Everything won't always be perfect, but through animal communications, you can help make the best decisions for you and your animal companions.

How animal communication helped rescue dog Stella to find the perfect home.

Just as you have considered what would make an ideal pet for you and your home, and you want to know that they are happy and settled in with you--

pets have considerations, too. Have you ever heard a pet parent say "They chose me," or "They rescued me!"? As the on-call animal communicator for a rescue center, I was asked to find out more from a dog who had been adopted into a "furever" home, but then returned after a short time. While rescued pets often have traumatic pasts, not all want to talk about them. However, this dog was quite clear as to why she couldn't settle into the new home.

It seemed that there had been miscommunication between Stella and the new parent. She was frightened of the noise and activity going on outside the home, and was barking because she was trying to tell the new owner she wanted to be inside. He didn't like her barking so much, so he returned her to the rescue. Stella was upset at the rejection, but didn't feel safe in the home. I asked her about the type of home she wanted so that she had a better chance of finding the right fit. She gave me her wish list for her perfect life in the perfect home, almost like a vision board. I relayed the information to the rescue team, and a short time later, they found Stella the perfect family and home.

How Wyatt the cat was able to cross the rainbow bridge under his own terms.

Cats are very stoic and amazing at hiding what is going on with them internally. As such, they often deteriorate quickly towards the end. Everything is fine, you are lulled into a false sense of security, and then suddenly things start happening all at once. Wyatt was a trooper; however, he was becoming ill, and the list of ailments kept growing. Finally, his vet determined that there was nothing else they could do. Wyatt's mom reached out to me, asking what to do.

Usually I need a photo for remote animal communication; however, I already knew Wyatt, so I was able to connect with him to share information between him and his mom. I stayed in touch throughout the next few days to help the family and Wyatt through the transition. Wyatt wanted to be at home, not at the vet's office. He was also ready to move on, but was waiting for certain people to come and say goodbye. The in-home euthanasia went smoothly, and Wyatt came through to me right afterwards to let his mom know he was thankful and all was well.

So, what if you could know your pet's thoughts and wishes? Would you be surprised by what they were? It can be frustrating trying to understand your animal's body language. Are they hungry, sad, annoyed, in pain? Maybe they weren't looking to go out, but instead they wanted you to get their favorite toy that's been missing under the couch for a while and now they want to play with it. Maybe they just needed a hug.

Are you ready to learn what your pets are trying to tell you? Animal communication can be a key to understanding your pet's needs, and help you to make the right decisions for you and your pets. I'd love to help you build that stronger bond and relationship with them; therefore, I have created a special page on my website just for you at www. FourPawsHolisticTherapy.com/jumpstart. There, you will find tips and opportunities to create that special bond and be able to schedule a free consultation with me!

About the Author

Gillian H. Edwards

A Certified Animal Communicator, Karuna/Reiki Master, Canine Massage Practitioner, and instructor at the Rocky Mountain School of Animal Acupressure and Massage, Gillian provides long-term big-picture holistic healing solutions for pets to activate their natural ability to balance and heal their physical, emotional, and mental well-being. With the belief that holistic therapy is centered on love, empathy, and respect, Gillian uses her knowledge and skills to help improve an animal's health and happiness, which can strengthen and deepen their connections to their human companions.

Jumpstart Your Business Chapters

Jumpstart Your Bookkeeping

Why and How to Do Everything Virtually

By Nicole Anderson

You know that sinking feeling when your computer crashes, and you get the "blue screen of death," or your laptop is lost or stolen, and you had EVERYTHING on the C:\ drive?

Well, with today's technology and cloud-based software, there is no reason why this should ever happen again.

After 25 years in corporate accounting, I was so tired of sitting in a cubicle and being chained to my desk. I wanted more freedom and control of my time and my life. When I was laid off from my last corporate job, it was a blessing in disguise. I did not know the first thing about starting my own business, but I jumped in with both feet and started my remote bookkeeping business in 2019.

Since speaking with or working directly with hundreds of small business owners, I have learned that most small business owners need some basic guidance in financial education in order to build their businesses to the level they want, and be able to enjoy the profits they deserve.

Financial statements are the story of your business. Make sure you can tell a good story. How do you know whether you're making a profit if you're not tracking income and expenses? That which is not being measured, cannot be improved. It's like baking a cake. If you don't measure what is going in, you have no idea what will come out.

The Three Financial Statements and How to Read Them

First, I need to give Intuit QuickBooks credit for this metaphor. I heard them explain the Three Financial Statements in this manner at a conference. So, think of the Three Financial Statements as an apple tree. The apples are your Profit and Loss statement, also known as the Income Statement. The trunk is the Balance Sheet. The roots are the Statement of Cash Flows, and the branches are all the people that need to read your statements: investors, bankers, and tax preparers. There will be years you have a good harvest, and other years you will not. You want to sell more apples (profit) than what hit the ground and rot (loss).

The **Profit and Loss** report tracks the business income and expenses by month, quarter, or annually. At the end of each year, the Net Income or Net Loss will move to the Balance Sheet as Retaining Earnings. Make sure you review this report monthly and check that your expenses are in line with your income.

The **Balance Sheet** reveals the health and stability of the business. This statement tracks the annual yields and company value. It also supports the business, just like the trunk of a tree.

The Balance Sheet is read as a point in time, usually at the end of the month, quarter, or year. It tells investors, bankers, and lenders that what your company OWNs, minus what your company OWEs, is the Value of your Business. Investors want to make sure that if they loan you money, they will get it back--plus interest.

The **Statement of Cash Flows** shows you where the money was absorbed into the company. Just like watering a tree, the roots need water, or "cash," to live. The tree needs water to thrive, and a business needs cash to grow. The Statement of Cash Flows will show you where that cash was spent based on three areas: operating, investing, or financing activities. This statement uses the information from both the Profit and Loss Sheet and the Balance Sheet to show you how this happened. The Statement of Cash Flows is the glue that ties the other two sheets together.

Which online accounting system is right for you to house the data that produces these statements?

There are plenty of online, cloud-based accounting software options available these days. You need to review your business needs in order to determine what software will work for you. The top 4 options are Sage 40/Simply Accounting (formerly Peachtree), AccountEdge Pro, Xero and QuickBooks Online. For the clients I serve, I find that QuickBooks Online (QBO) is the best option. In my experience, this is the most versatile software to serve any business from the small business start-up to the large brick and mortar business. QBO has over 700 add-on apps to cover anything you may need the system to do to support your business needs.

There are five subscription levels: Self-Employed, Simple Start, Essential, Plus, and Advanced. I don't recommend Self-Employed because it's housed on a different platform, so if you wish to upgrade at a later date, it will be challenging. If you sign up for QBO through your bookkeeper, you can get the monthly subscription for 50% off for the life of the plan. As a QBO Pro-Advisor, I can help you get the wholesale rate, thus saving you money.

When comparing QuickBooks Online (QBO) vs. QuickBooks Desktop, the number one reason to select the online option is access. You get real-time access to your business information from your laptop, phone, and tablet. Plus, you will have the benefit of shared access with your bookkeeper and CPA without uploading files to Dropbox or a jump drive. The software is regularly updated with the latest improvements, and your data is in the cloud. No need to back up your computer.

Online Banking – STOP Writing Checks

Even the smallest of banks and credit unions have online apps and platforms to do your banking on the go. I have not yet come across a bank that doesn't link to QBO. All of your transactions are pulled into the software; simply tell the system which type of expense or income to log for any particular transaction. I highly recommend retaining your monthly bank statements in order to reconcile your account. You can pay all your vendors, employees, and contractors via Automatic Clearing House (ACH). No additional app or add-on is needed. Vendors and employees are paid within 24 hours. You will not have to deal with lost checks, and it's easier to reconcile your bank account monthly.

Online Data Storage (Go Paperless)

I love hubdoc.com. You can link your bank accounts and store all of your business documents in one place. The system will download the documents and file them for you—no need to log into your bank accounts monthly. Also, you can email receipts or upload them from your phone or computer. You won't ever misplace your receipts again. Everything is properly filed and safely stored in the cloud. You can also scan receipts on your phone directly into QBO. QBO will pick up the amount, the date, and other legible information from the receipt, making it a one stop shop for attaching receipts to the bank transactions.

Collecting Payments from Customers

There are lots of online payment solutions out there today. Stripe is the leading online payment software. If Shopify powers your online store, Shopify will process credit card payments without a 3rd party payment provider. Square, PayPal, Cash App, and Venmo are just a few online payment solutions. The downside of these 3rd party payment solutions is that when they hit the bank account, they only read "Venmo" or "PayPal." The transaction doesn't tell you exactly where the money came from or who paid you. Zelle, another digital payment network, does note the payee in the accounting system, which is super helpful. If you have monthly recurring subscription clients, you can set up an auto-debit within QBO. Your client won't need to remember to pay you, and you will have fewer worries about falling behind on your accounts receivable.

What's Next?

Keep your books clean. Make it a habit, like checking your email. Take 5 minutes every morning, or at least weekly, to update your banking transactions and post them to the appropriate account. Five minutes now, will save you so much time and headache at year-end. Review your reports quarterly with your CPA to make sure you don't need to make quarterly estimated tax payments. If you are tracking your mileage manually, post that daily or weekly too.

Hire a Bookkeeper!

If you genuinely hate numbers and the idea of looking at your accounting software makes you want to throw up, then it's worth the money to hire a bookkeeper that LOVES numbers and enjoys working online every morning.

Whether it's me or someone else, we can create a process for you and your business. Utilizing my expertise, I will keep you on track and work with your

CPA or tax preparer to make sure you are looking good.

Focus on your business; let the bookkeeper worry about the paperwork. If you can keep the day-to-day activities caught up, terrific! However, please hire a CPA for taxes. This will be money well spent. No one has time for an audit. The CPA and bookkeeper can both access your online accounting system. By enlisting help with all of this, you'll.have real-time, up-to-date books.

Oh my, I have so much more I would like to share with you. Please visit www.Excellent-Bookkeeping. com/jumpstart for up-to-date information and my list of the Top 10 Tax Tips, plus a book on other software recommendations that I couldn't fit into this chapter: a special gift to you for reading my chapter. I hope you have learned something today, and I hope I have helped you "Excel Your P&L."

By Nicole Anderson

About the Author
Nicole Anderson

Nicole Anderson, owner of Excellent Bookkeeping Services, LLC, is passionate about helping you to EXCEL your P&L. She has worked in diverse corporate accounting roles for 25+ years. Today, she uses her corporate knowledge and Bachelors in Accounting to support service-based entrepreneurs through QuickBooks Online. Most importantly, Nicole's goal is to make sure YOU feel CONFIDENT with your accounting processes and procedures.

Jumpstart Your Business

8 Secrets to Building a Consistent Money-Making Business

By Katrina Sawa

I want you to close your eyes for a minute—just humor me—and paint a picture in your mind. It's three years, two years, or even just one year from now, and you have a consistent money-making business. That business is providing everything you need for your family, and you're not killing yourself working 24/7 to have it, either. In fact, you're working your ideal hours, helping your ideal clients and customers.

This can be your future if you take the time now to do what it takes to set up your foundation. If you're an entrepreneur now, or you want to be one, this chapter will share the main areas of what you will need to focus on to get what you want and to be where you want.

I've owned my own business since 2002, and before that, all of my jobs that I've held were involving some sort of sales or marketing. I majored in it in college, and I've held all sorts of positions at various companies. I've even sold door-to-door! I know what it takes to sell stuff and make money. I've been very good at it, and just like the saying goes, I fully believe that "selling is serving." You have to believe that the thing you offer is worth what you're charging (or more), and then you have to pursue those who need it. You have to be assertive, and not back down. Be proud and loud about what you have to offer!

Let me share with you the 8 Secrets to a Consistent Money-Making Business that I've found to be true, and could help you too.

Secret #1: Know your Big Picture Vision and your Goals; Believe it's Possible.

I have found that many of my clients choose to work on goal planning and vision only once or twice a year. They set their Big Vision, and perhaps even design a Vision Board. Visioning can be a daily practice. Pairing it with your morning meditation is a surefire way to ensure success.

So, what does your Big Vision look like? As you make more and more money, your vision may change and grow, and you will be able to do better in the world with that additional income.

Secret #2: Develop the Right Pricing and Offerings for You and Your Ideal Lifestyle.

"What are you selling?" It is imperative for you to be clear on what specific products and services you offer through your business. What you're selling to your prospect, though, is the "transformation" that those products and services provide. What will be the outcome for them if (or when) they buy and use your products and services?

If you are not 100% clear on what you are selling, or its price point, then you need to get clear. When you don't have absolute clarity on your offer, it will be much harder to close the sale.

Whatever you offer, please make sure you charge "enough." Too many entrepreneurs don't charge enough because they don't believe they're worth it. Maybe you don't think you're worth a higher rate, because you haven't been "in the business long enough." Or perhaps you over-deliver by fixing additional problems and issues to the ones for which you're being paid to fix—but you're not charging extra for the additional work.

Secret #3: Exude Massive Confidence to Attain Positive Expert Positioning.

Confidence comes with clarity, and clarity comes with knowing exactly what you're selling and for how much. Knowing your price point will help you to sell your wares with complete confidence because, if you've done your research and you know what you're worth, then you will stand tall and tell your potential new client what your price is, and you won't just automatically give a discount. Often, growing in confidence is just a matter of one or two clients paying you at a certain rate and then you have proof. I tell my own clients to charge as much as you can possibly say out loud without stuttering. When you can tell a potential client, "My coaching is $300 an hour," with a smile on your face and your chin up, then you're well on your way.

Secret #4: Implement Smart, Consistent, Yet Ever-Evolving Marketing Practices.

When you're marketing, you need to be implementing more than just one or two strategies. In fact, I teach 20+ different marketing strategies in my workshops. You need to be open to trying new things such as video marketing. More than half of my clients aren't excited about doing videos, but they work and they do them anyway. If you hate social media and think it's a waste of time but you know your target market is hanging out there, then you have to figure out how to be there too, in order to be visible to them. You can hire a Virtual Assistant to do the things you know you need to do but either don't like to do, don't know how to do, or don't want to do yourself.

Marketing is primarily about relationships and building community. You want to join some communities for networking and collaborations, and you may even want to lead a community so YOU can become the expert influencer. Find your way and what works for you and your business, your clients, and your personality, but don't avoid something just because you don't like it.

Secret #5: Enlist Systems, Strategies, and a Team to Stay Organized.

This step is a little more difficult for "control freaks." You think it's just easier for you to do everything rather than take a moment to teach someone else how to do something in your business. It may take longer in the short run, but in the long run, you'll be able to leave your business for weeks and still bring in revenue when you have the right systems and team. For example—if you spend too much time doing administrative tasks, bookkeeping, and follow-up by yourself, then you might be missing out on making more sales.

Systems aren't necessarily technologies; they are processes or strategies for how something will get done. You want procedures for each area of your business, whether it's marketing, follow-up, data entry, advertising, product delivery and shipping, etc. Without a plan, you're certainly wasting time and money. And having a team can mean hiring independent contractors, for limited hours and minimal expense. Delegating allows for you to spend your time on the things that you do best.

Step #6: Embrace the Right Technology to Make Your Life Easier.

Technology can certainly help to save you time and keep you organized. Utilizing technology to simplify your business could be as simple as tracking clients and potential clients in an Excel spreadsheet, or the implementation of online banking. One thing that most business owners will need is an email marketing software to keep in touch with your customers. Another is having a shopping cart or payment processor...you can't be successful if you don't make money, and you want to make it really easy for your clients to pay you. In addition, things like Google Calendar and other scheduling software can keep you on task. I live by my calendar.

Secret #7: Sustain a Positive Money Mindset with Swift Money-Making Decisions

Try to be mindful of how you speak about money. Rather than focusing on scarcity and speaking about money in a negative way (e.g. "I can't afford that."), shift your mindset and say, "How CAN I afford this?" instead.

In addition, when evaluating monetary decisions, do it quickly and with your full attention. Don't let the decision linger, because your hesitancy is negative energy. Give the investment opportunity your full focus, feel it in your gut, make the decision, and tweak it as you go if you need to. I like to say, "Money follows speed!"

Secret #8: Don't Settle for Anything Less than 100% Personal Happiness, Love, and Support.

This is the glue that holds everything together. If you are settling anywhere in your life, your business, your job, your relationship—this is toxic to your entrepreneurial energy. Only with the proper love and support in your personal life, can you achieve full potential in your business. Things are going to happen in life: people go through hard times, illness, loss of family and friends, natural disasters, and poor decisions that result in terrible outcomes. But if your foundation is strong, if your support system is there, then you will get through. Protect your positive energy and try really hard to avoid negative people.

Follow these steps, and you, too, can create a business that continues to make money every month. Thanks to these 8 Secrets, my business runs smoothly and pulls in money whether I'm ill, on vacation, or working at the top of my game. This has been possible because I took the time to set up my business the right way from the start, and because I continue to invest in myself, my training, getting support from mentors, and hiring a team.

I want you to succeed as I have, so please go grab some of my free resources that I've put for you on this page on my site: www.JumpstartYourBizNow. com/freetrainings.

About the Author
Katrina Sawa

Katrina Sawa is an award-winning international speaker and business coach known as the JumpStart Your Biz Coach, because she kicks her clients and their businesses into high gear! She is the creator of the JumpStart Your Marketing® System, Jumpstart Your Business System, and Int'l Best-Selling Author with 11 books. She loves to inspire and educate other entrepreneurs on how to create a consistent money-making business doing what they love.

Jumpstart Your Efficiency

3 Keys to Increasing Your Profits

By Tina Palmgren

You're sitting at your computer, downloading your bank transactions so you can verify yesterday's bank deposits in your bank account against those your system shows for yesterday's deposits. You have to manipulate the bank data into a format that you can use, just like you did yesterday, and the day before that. Every time you begin this task, you have to widen columns, add totals, delete columns and rows, change the font, set up as a table...all to make the file ready to work with.

While you are manipulating the data in order to analyze it – the phone is ringing. Emails are popping up, demanding your attention and adding to your never-ending list of things you must do today. You say to yourself, "This is a pain in the ass!" while secretly thinking, "There MUST be a better way to do this." But this is how we've always done it.

In my 27 years of accounting, I've worked the full gamut of business. I have experience with everything from small businesses with one employee to large corporations with over 20,000 employees. Within this variety of business models, I began to notice patterns of inefficiency and inaccuracy. Because two of my core values are accuracy and efficiency, and I am a rebel at heart, I would simply take it upon myself to fix things without going through the proper channels. Wasting time sitting in unproductive meetings where no one listened to me anyway, really annoyed me. Sometimes, it's better to ask for forgiveness than to ask for permission!

Are you too busy running your business processes to add any new clients? Are you burning the candle at both ends working late again? You're not alone if you answered yes to either of these questions.

What if I could show you how to free up an extra 6.5 weeks this year? That's exactly what I did for one client I worked with. I developed a process for their shipping department, which was struggling with determining the correct number of parts being shipped each day. They had constant errors. The process I created made it crystal clear where the errors were, allowing the shipping personnel to correct the errors before the parts were shipped out.

The accuracy in the number of parts shipped saved over an hour per day in Accounts Payable. That's five hours EACH week, totaling over 20 hours per month. That's 260 hours per year, which is a total of 6.5 weeks EVERY year. That equated to over $10,000 saved each year.

Regardless of whether you even have a shipping department or not, imagine what you could do with 6.5 extra weeks and a savings of $10,000 per year. What systems and processes could we make more efficient for YOU? I want you to really think about what your time is worth to you.

The BIG question is: What are you doing today to achieve the vision you have for your business? It's the small steps we take today that create the BIG changes we want for our future.

As entrepreneurs and small business owners, we're busy people, wearing many hats. We do the work of 20. Can you relate? We don't have the luxury of time, and sometimes there are parts of our business we don't enjoy doing. Let's face it, not everything in business is our cup of tea. For me, that's doing my own taxes; it drains all my energy to even think about it. But to make our business successful, there are things we need to do to ensure our success--and not go to jail!

Our businesses need to be accurate, efficient, and making a profit, or we won't be in business very long.

Sometimes we can't see the forest for the trees. We're so busy working our business that we don't always see what's not working, or know how to make the changes to improve our bottom line--much less have the time or energy to figure it out.

I've found that, although each business is unique, there are common business principles we all follow, and there are patterns of dysfunction that eat into our profits.

Unfortunately, most business owners don't see them, because they're doing business the way they always have, operating under practices that may have been a great idea when they were formed...but not much so anymore.

I want to share with you the 3 Keys to Increasing Your Profits, because it breaks my heart when I see processes that have errors, that waste people's time, that zap all your energy, or that are tedious.

1. **Errors** - Relying on inaccurate data leads to poor decisions, creates unnecessary steps, causes frustration, wastes time, and results in lost profits.

   A millwright company I worked for shortly after I was out of college had no system in place to track the equipment used on job sites unless it was rented. Every time I went to bill for time and material jobs, I needed to ask the project manager what equipment was used. How good is your memory from two weeks ago? (Spoiler: This is not an accurate way of billing.)

   I created a 3-part form that tracked all the equipment used for each job. The shop had a copy, so they knew where the equipment was; the foreman had a copy, so he knew what equipment needed to be returned to the shop; and the job file had a copy, for billing the client. Besides not having equipment "walk away" from the jobsite, the form increased our billing revenue by 15% within the first year, equaling an additional $150,000.

Can you think of any areas where you may be letting money walk out the door?

2. **Re-keying Data** – Having to type data into a second spot is just asking for trouble. Not only is it a giant waste of time, but let's face it, we are all human and we all make mistakes.

One client I worked with was keying data from an Excel spreadsheet into a Word document to print out sale tags, which they posted in their stores each month. It took them approximately eight hours every month to do this process.

Using a simple automated system I created for them, the process is now completed in less than 3 minutes from start to finish, with a simple click of the mouse.

This saves them 7 hours and 57 minutes *every month!* That's a time savings of 2.5 weeks a year, and there are no typos to deal with!

Do you have any current processes that include re-keying data from one place to another?

3. **Repetitive Tasks** – I commonly see businesses lose time and profits in manually processing repetitive tasks and reports. Automating your information is the key to eliminating this problem. To relieve us of the time consuming and tedious task of manually manipulating data, like the download of the bank deposit transactions I talked about earlier, automation increases both productivity and accuracy, by eliminating your need to do the work.

I worked for a health care provider that had 10 hospitals, and each hospital had their own spreadsheet. Every day, someone had to manually copy all the unposted transactions from each of the eight tabs onto one tab so it could be transferred to the next day's spreadsheet. Copying and pasting all the unposted records took 20 minutes per hospital - IF there were no errors! Automating the process instantly copies all the transactions to one sheet, so now it can be quickly filtered to find the day's unposted transactions. These unposted transactions are now copied all at once to another tab, so they can easily be added to the next day's spreadsheet.

The automated system copies all the data from each tab, and is done in less than 3 seconds. 20 minutes times 10 hospitals is 200 minutes per day, which is a savings of more than three hours per day, 15 hours per week, 780 hours, or 19.5 weeks, per year!

In dollar values, 780 x 18.00 per hour = $14,040 in savings per year.

Think about the tasks that you repeat – daily, weekly, monthly, or even yearly. How could you benefit from automating your repetitive tasks?

My super-power is finding easier, more efficient ways to do things. I need to know the "why" behind a process, because I love making it quicker and easier with no errors. Using your current process, together we automate and customize what you are already doing so there isn't a lot of change in what's done-- just how you do it. You created the original system and still know how it works. But now it is automated so that anyone can run it and not mess it up, making it easy to delegate the process.

If you'd like to have a conversation to review your business systems and figure out ways to excel your business profits and save you time, then sign up for a complimentary Systems Flow Assessment with me. This assessment is totally free for those of you reading this chapter, but please don't wait. All my clients wish they had hired me sooner. **Sign up now at www.ExcelingYourBusiness.com/Efficiency.**

About the Author
Tina Palmgren

Tina is an Efficiency Expert who transforms your time-consuming, tedious tasks into quick and easy solutions--with a little sass on the side! As a speaker, she knows how to incorporate humor and engage her audience. Working in several different industries has developed Tina's abilities to find errors and create efficiencies in every department. Tina is a former Excel professor at both UWSP and Rasmussen College. She carries a BA in Accounting and an MBA in Technology Management.

Jumpstart Your Follow-Up

5 Ways to Keep in Touch with Prospects

By Lisa DeToffol

When I started my business two years ago, I was unaware of the importance of following up with prospects and clients. Through observation of how building relationships and staying in contact with your audience, prospects, and clients are vital to growing a business, I realized a Follow-Up system was key.

You may be enjoying good success because of your hard work, aspirations, and selling skills. Your feature-rich product/service can also be a beneficial factor in achieving good results. But there is one key ingredient to dramatically improving your sales...it's consistent follow-up.

Following up on prospects is a critical step in building and maintaining long-term relationships. It involves a simple communication effort to gauge customer interest, understand their problems, and identify the primary problems for which they might be seeking solutions. Without following up with the prospects to figure out their needs, businesses cannot understand whether their products/services are the best solutions for their customers/clients.

As business owners, one of our challenges is following up with potential clients after providing information about what we have to offer. It is easy to assume, when you haven't heard back from a contact, that they don't care to work with you or they have found a better offer. Maybe your pricing is too high, or you didn't present the information well, etc. By making these assumptions and not following up at least 12 times or more, you could be leaving money on the table.

Don't leave your follow-up to chance. Most business owners fail to invest in setting and communicating clear expectations for what good follow-up actually looks like beyond some vague generalities. GET SPECIFIC! Create a follow-up schedule that outlines when you'll make your calls or send emails. The goal is to maintain appropriate, timely follow-up processes no matter whether they're ready to sign a contract today or ask you to call them back in two months. Follow-up schedules can and should extend all the way out to 12 months, although the tenor and frequency of communications should change significantly as time goes on and based on the level of interest displayed from the prospect. Mapping out a follow-up schedule means that no lead will fall through the cracks.

In today's society, your clients crave relationships...a connection...an impact on their lives. With that in mind, here are 5 forms of "Follow-Up" you can implement into your business that will give your customers/clients what they crave.

1. **Phone Calls** - Reach out by phone: leave a message, or talk to the person and let them know you appreciate them and their business, and look forward to working with them again soon. Follow-up calls are essential to the sales cycle. A sales follow-up call has the power to establish a relationship with the prospect. You can probe more by asking relevant questions to learn about their problems and understand their situation. Be genuinely interested in helping them with their problems. If you can't close the deal, at least you will have a richer knowledge base with which to better serve others in their buying cycles.

2. **Emails** - Reconnect with those who have visited your website, attended your event, or responded to your offer. Let them know you are happy that they visited, and offer to help them with the service you provide from which they could benefit. Offer to schedule a phone call for a more detailed discussion, during which you can answer any question they may have. There is a thin line between sending a good follow-up email that is actually going to help you, and being annoying. Follow-up should bring constant value and keep your prospect moving through the buying cycle.

3. **Social Media** - After a meeting or event, take time to connect through social media with prospects you met or with whom you came into contact at the event. Check out all their social media pages, and follow or like them. While you are there, explore a little bit about what they post, and to

whom they are speaking. Add that information to your follow-up notes in case it is relevant to your conversation. Social Media is meant to be social, so don't just follow them and be done with it. Take the opportunity to reach out and send them a personal message. Like and share their content often, if you share their content, they will share yours. Also, interact with them when they comment on a post on your page, and offer to connect with them further to learn about each other's businesses and answer any questions that arise throughout the conversation.

4. **Personal Note** - How does it make you feel to receive a thank you card in the mail? Cards are the key to appreciation in the business world. A card gets 100% open rate vs. bills or emails. Cards help you to remain in a potential client's mind, and make you Stand Out above others; cards touch people in many ways. Cards are personal. Mary Kay sends handwritten cards to clients to make them feel important and let them know someone cares about them. You could send 3 cards a week to 3 different prospective clients to express appreciation for their business or connection.

5. **Referrals** - Happy and satisfied customers/clients will always refer your products/services to their friends, colleagues, and associates. When a recommendation comes from someone who has actually used your service/product, it has an extra layer of credibility and trust. Delighted clients/customers are the best advocates, because third party claims of excellence carry more weight than self-promotion. Most clients/customers are always willing to refer, because they know how important referrals are in the business world.

The fortune is in the Follow-Up!

You may have heard that saying, and it's true.

Why spend your time networking if you are not going to do the additional work to make those connections stronger? And when you develop a system that works for you, your follow-up can be flawless and consistent.

You can use different forms to follow up. It's as simple as it sounds. Use more than one way to reach out. The goal is to connect with prospects in different ways in order to stay at the front of their minds and stand out from the competition. Get a hold of people in whatever way that works. Think outside the BOX!

Remember, at the beginning of the buying process, you will have spent some time scoping out your prospects. During this time, you should try to get an understanding of their buying habits. Is this potential client someone who is likely to act quickly? Or will he or she need lots of information and encouragement? This research will help you to plan your follow-up tactics with each particular client. Traditionally, most follow-up is done manually. Following a presentation, you may ask prospects whether they are ready to make a decision.

A week or two later, you may give them a call and ask them the same question. What many business people don't realize is that you need to follow up more than once or twice. In fact, sometimes you may need to follow up as many as 12 times. But not every instance of follow-up needs to be a manual call asking for the sale. It could be a reminder about a fast-action discount that will soon be expiring, a newsletter with some client testimonials, or an informational sheet demonstrating the value that you offer. You can get creative in the ways that you choose to keep in contact with prospective clients, and get them used to your outreach. In the process, you will be building relationships with them and demonstrating the value of your business to them. Just remember, communication is a big factor when following up.

How do you express appreciation and stay connected? A tool I use is a simple greeting card and an occasional gift. The card I send allows me to personalize the message, add my own handwritten signature, and include photos of the recipient. People have told me how they keep the cards on display for frequent viewing.

By using the correct channels of communication, you are building rapport and a relationship. This is exactly what you want. To help your business grow in the right direction, you must have great communication. To build great relationships, you will need to have the proper follow-up system in place, to help nurture those relationships and continue to grow your business.

If you know that you need to do more follow-up marketing but realize that you need some help to do it, reach out! I'd love to see how I can help you grow your business by staying in touch with your prospects, clients, and referral sources on a consistent basis. At Tiger Eye Solution, we are passionate about helping you succeed. Our Certified Virtual Expert® Services will allow you to focus on what you do best, while we do what we do best.

For a FREE guide on Follow-Up for Speakers, Coaches, and Small Business Owners, go to my website at www.tigereyesolution.com/jumpstart and you'll get a checklist for the 7 Secrets to Following Up with Prospects.

About the Author
Lisa DeToffol

Lisa DeToffol is a Certified Virtual Expert® Specializing in Relationship Management and Follow-Up. She is certified by the Virtual Expert® Training Program. Lisa supports Speakers, Coaches, and Small Business Owners by keeping them on current and prospective clients' radars. As a former teacher, she is extremely creative and organized. She is a wife and mother, with dreams of making a difference in the lives and businesses of others.

Jumpstart Your HR Department

7 Steps to a Smoother-Running, Employee-Based Business

By Amber Trail

Wait! Don't skip this chapter because you think you don't need to learn about HR!!

Regardless of whether you think you NEED an HR Department in your business, company, or organization, you will. Trust me.

Having an HR Department is not just for big corporations. It's for the smallest of businesses, too. Do you know why? Because THEY are the ones who get targeted and sued due to firing, negligence, and unlawful discrimination cases. Even if you have a business with ONE employee, you will want to get all of these 7 areas in check.

Let me share why, and then I'll share what you can do about it.

First off, I had no idea that I would ever be a Human Resources professional. My dislike of HR came early on in my corporate career. I had been sexually harassed in my very first job, which I had actually loved. I wasn't supported by the company or their HR department at all, and the lack of support resulted in my decision to leave the company.

I had always felt that HR was just there for legal reasons, and was not really of any use for the employees. It turns out that this idea was the result of a few "bad egg" experiences that left a terrible feeling in the pit of my stomach whenever I heard the words "human resources." A former coworker of mine had worked in HR for a while, and she helped me to realize that Human Resources was there to be a mediator and a coach between employer and employee.

What is Human Resources? Well, I could spend hours upon hours researching the definitions found in Google, but I'll spare you. During my time in HR, I can sum it up in one sentence. Human Resources helps the workforce to excel by creating a fulfilling culture, while abiding by legal compliance. Basically, an HR professional ensures the safety of the workplace, the hiring/firing of employees, documentation, proper training(s), and the like.

Now, with all of that being said, how do you Jumpstart your HR Department? If you currently don't have an HR Department or haven't even spoken to an HR professional or consultant yet in your business, you definitely want to read on. If you do have one, but maybe you realize it needs an overhaul, please read on.

This chapter will review the Top 7 Tips for Creating or Redefining your HR Department in a matter of a few days.

Step 1: Company Handbook.

This is a must for a company with any number of employees. It manages and maintains the guidelines that lay out the processes, culture, and policies suitable to your specific business needs. No policy is effective if it is practiced inconsistently. Handbooks provide consistent and clear guidelines to follow in most situations that occur within the workplace. We know they aren't the most enjoyable reading material out there, but they protect both the employer and the employee. And that's a big deal for HR.

A handbook includes all of the policies, procedures, expectations (particularly behavioral), agreements, and even the mission and values of the business, and it is completely catered to your business. This handbook and the signed statement will be vital to fighting unemployment or any EEOC claims that may occur, as long as you follow your own guidelines. Speaking of which, be a role model to your employees, and don't behave as if the handbook policies do not apply to you. News flash: they apply to everyone.

In my years of HR experience, no business operates in the same way, and every handbook is customized accordingly and appropriately.

Step 2: Personnel Files and I-9s.

It's extremely rare to find someone who likes their privacy being exposed – am I right, or am I right? Do yourself and your employees a huge favor, and keep all personnel files and I-9s private and well-documented.

All personnel files should be kept in a locked cabinet away from roaming employees. Limit access to only a few key leadership members.

I-9s should always be kept separate from current employee files.

Never keep copies of a social security card, birth certificate, or passport.

Organize your personnel files in a way that makes sense.

Section 1: Resume / Application / Background Check

Section 2: Tax Forms / Direct Deposit

Section 3: Health Insurance Forms / 401k Forms

Section 4: Performance Appraisals / Disciplinary Action

Terminated employee files should be filed away separately from the active employee files.

Terminated employee I-9s should be kept in a separate file and disposed of according to the IRS guidelines.

Step 3: Listening Skills.

The mutual respect that is highly desirable for many business owners, leadership teams, and employees begins with listening. Sometimes, listening is more powerful than speaking. Listen to what your employees want and need. Listen to their concerns and suggestions. And be someone with whom your employees feel comfortable discussing private matters.

Reinventing your business starts with your people. Take care of them and in turn, they'll take care of you.

Step 4: Compliance.

Do you know what your state and county guidelines are? Do you know what the federal guidelines are? Keeping up with new laws and ever-changing guidelines can be difficult, if not just completely overwhelming. But being up-to-date with compliance prevents any potential fines (and boy can they be costly), as well as other penalties.

Join a group such as the Society of Human Resource Management to keep up with the newest updates.

Step 5: Performance Reviews.

Why is a performance review so important? Employees need feedback. They need to know how to improve. Create goals for them to accomplish. Let them know where their strengths are, and give them the tools they need to enhance their weaknesses. You wouldn't want to coast through a job without knowing how you're doing, would you? Performance reviews can actually be a fantastic motivational resource for employees, not only because they constructively know what they can improve upon, but because their strengths are being noticed and acknowledged.

Performance reviews should be conducted on a yearly basis. New hires should have a review after 30 days, and again after 90 days. This is a great time to visit any possible raises/bonuses with employees, or even to discuss concerns and other issues from either party that need to be addressed.

Step 6: Training.

Training is vital in any organization. You can't expect someone, on their first day or even within their first month, to know exactly how to do their job without some type of training. That's inefficient, and a waste of time and energy for everyone.

The world is filled with a variety of training options. Pick a few that will increase the productivity of your workforce. Provide leadership training, safety training, productivity, diversity, and of course, sexual harassment training to your employees. When you put the time and effort into your workforce, your rewards as a business owner can last a lifetime.

Step 7: Hire an HR Consultant.

Small businesses sometimes don't have the need for a full-time HR staff member. That's where HR Consultants come in. Using a consultant can be a much more affordable option to many business owners when tackling necessary HR tasks. Sometimes, just getting your HR department set up is the most important step when following federal and state guidelines. Let someone with experience and knowledge help you.

Human Resources is vital to any organization with employees. When you set up your department, or revamp it, it sets a tone of professionalism, respect, and trust. Small business owners are busy--trust me, I know--but you can't do it all. In my professional experience, you sometimes learn that you need to hire those who are experts in their field, which may also be a field in which you are challenged. Don't exhaust yourself by taking on everything. Reach out to professionals to help you with whatever challenge you are facing, and remember to be kind to yourself and to others.

Trust me when I say that your employees will work harder, go the extra mile, and do whatever it takes to watch your company grow and succeed, when they see that they are important in your eyes. They matter.

Are you ready to Jumpstart your HR Department?

We are here to help! **I want to give you a Free eBook for you to get started.** Go right now and check this out, so you can begin the important task of developing and restructuring your HR department. **You can find the eBook on a special page on my website just for you, www.TheHRTrail.com/ jumpstart.** If you're looking for a powerful team of supportive and brilliant HR professionals to help you with even the smallest task for revamping your whole HR department, please contact us for a free consultation. We always provide phenomenal information on our blog posts, which can be found on our website at www.TheHRTrail.com.

About the Author
Amber Trail

Amber Trail, MBA, SHRM-CP, is the Founder and Consultant of The HR Trail, LLC, and the Founder of the Empowered Professionals Group. Amber brings in over a decade of experience and has created the perfect blend of business expertise and empathy. Amber decided to reinvent businesses through their people. Empowering employees to do more and be more, creates a powerful workforce for each employer who is looking to retain their top talent.

Jumpstart Your Influence

4 Keys to Making a Bigger Impact

By Katrina Sawa

I want you to be ridiculously successful in whatever you plan to do. This means that you'll probably need to learn some new skills along the way. You definitely need to learn how to be a better speaker and business person if you run your own business. You will want to be a better leader and an influencer if you plan to do big things in life or in your career. Anytime is a great time to learn tips on how to become a bigger or better Influencer.

"Influence" is one of those words that I never thought about too much, until about ten years into my business. That's when I began hearing my speaker peers and friends mention it during their talks, calls, and emails.

At first, I felt like, to be "an influencer," you had to be famous, such as a celebrity, singer, or actor.

When I stopped to think about it a few years back, about what having influence truly meant, I was excited to discover that I'd been doing many of the right things to BUILD INFLUENCE all throughout my entrepreneurial journey.

These days, I feel like anyone can be an influencer. You can be an influencer in your company, your niche, your industry, or even in your family or community.

For example, how many YouTubers have you seen go viral with ONE video, and now have millions of subscribers and followers?

What about the blogger or Instagram person who just started sharing their content or their opinion, and suddenly had hundreds of thousands of followers?

Those people have gone after endorsement opportunities or found sponsors for their blogs, and now they get PAID to share!

Now, these are rare occasions I think, as it does take quite a bit of work to become a bigger influencer. But with the Internet and social media on our side, being an influencer may not be that unattainable anymore.

In fact, there are negative influencers out there; you've seen them. They are the women showing their bodies on social media, for example, who have millions of followers, or the narcissists spouting political jargon who get millions of views or likes online. Some of the WRONG people are becoming influencers in our society for sure; therefore, we need more positive content creators to stand up and become bigger influencers if we truly want the world to be a better place.

You don't have to be an influencer ONLINE, unless that's your thing, but being an influencer, regardless of your industry or profession, can be a very rewarding experience. Think of being an influencer as being a thought leader. Thought leaders are more of a household name, such as Oprah Winfrey, Eckart Tolle, or Gandhi.

You and I can be influencers, too. You don't have to have millions of followers on Facebook or Instagram. You don't have to be making millions of dollars, either. You just need to have a message that others believe in; they have to like, trust, and connect with you, even if they never actually meet you.

We can be influencers in our families, and inspire our kids to be good kids and do good things. Setting a great example for them is sometimes all it takes.

We can be influencers in our communities and volunteer, lead rallies, or even start a bigger movement for a cause greater than our own.

Think about some of your favorite TV shows, podcasts, or radio shows. Many of the people on them were nobodies, until they were discovered!

Influencers can be people who provide a targeted type of content for a specific audience, like freelance journalists, bloggers, video YouTubers, and social media experts. An influencer can be anyone who masters a certain skill or craft, and then teaches it to others, such as a software platform, social media platform, or a specific life, health, or business strategy or process. Typically, Influencers become authors, speakers, and frequently show up on social media.

Here are a few reasons you may want to strive to be more of an influencer:

- Reach a bigger or broader audience for your message, your business, or your movement. *You could change a lot of lives!*

- Build more credibility, respect, and trust for yourself.

- Create fame and fortune (this is not everyone's goal, but this could happen!).

Definition of INFLUENCE:

The capacity to have an effect on the character, development, or behavior of someone or something, or the effect itself.

So where do you start? What can you do to grow your influence?

I've identified 4 Keys to Making a Bigger Impact by Jumpstarting Your Influence:

1. Build a Loyal Community of Followers

2. Be a Leader

3. Build Credibility

4. Share, Educate, and Inspire Often

You want to have people tell you, "I see you everywhere!" or "I hear your name everywhere!"

Let's talk about each one of these independently...

1. **Build a loyal community of followers** (wide and broad or narrow and deep) - As you're building your community, you want to nurture, educate, and inspire them. Often, they will follow you because you have a particular message, cause, or expertise that they want for themselves or that they can stand behind. Building a vast community requires massive marketing. You can impact change with a very small group of followers, but if you really want to make a huge difference, you will need to get in front of tens of thousands of people.

   - There are 3 different types of marketing on which every influencer focuses: New Business Marketing, Referral Source Marketing, and Database Marketing. Using all three of these will help you to get in front of thousands each month. (See Volume I of the Jumpstart Your ____ books for the Jumpstart Your Marketing chapter regarding this topic.) Regardless of whether or not you're trying to build your influence for the purpose of a business, becoming an Influencer still requires "marketing." You market when you hold a rally. You market when you entice your kids to eat all their vegetables by offering them their favorite dessert afterwards.

   - Think about how you want to inspire others; what legacy do you want to leave? What is YOUR bigger mission, purpose, or message with which you can be more of an influencer?

2. **Be a Leader** – You can set a better example and lead more in your business, with your employees, for your team, for your kids, and anyone else-- if you are more mindful. Building a following of people who like or love you, trust you, want to be around you, refer you, and/or take every training you've got to offer would be one result of your being a leader.

   - Leaders need to step up and do the right thing.

   - Leaders need to lead by example.

   - Leaders should show expertise, be both humble and confident, and be someone after which people want to model.

   - Leaders should be honest, loyal, and true to their word.

   - Think about how you lead, or whether you're really leading those who follow or look up to you.

3. **Build Credibility** - Credibility can be established and maintained through quite a few avenues. Here are a few things you can do:

   - You can write a book, which establishes you as an expert in the topic on which you write.

   - You can speak on your topic to groups of people, either virtually or in person.

   - You can host an event establishing you as the leading authority.

   - You can be interviewed on local or national television, radio shows, and podcasts, which elevates your expert status.

- You can start your own podcast or show of some kind, which really elevates your credibility.

- You can share success stories of your clients or followers.

- You can also pay to get in front of bigger audiences with television advertising, media coverage, and marketing - all of which make you look more important.

- What can you do today to build or showcase YOUR credibility?

4. **Share, Educate, and Inspire Often** - Influencers should (in my opinion) have the spirit of giving first. Finding all sorts of ways to give of your expertise, your content, your time, and your resources. This doesn't mean you have to give all your products and services away if you own your own business, but be that go-to-gal or go-to-guy to whom people reach out when they're looking for answers.

   - You want to provide great content, products, and programs.

   - You want to inspire and motivate those with whom you come into contact, regardless of whether they're paying you or not. It's about them remembering you, and how you impacted their life.

   - Think about in what ways you can give to and/or educate your followers.

I have put together a few free resources for you, so that you can start becoming a bigger influencer in your industry, life, family, and business. **Go to www.**

JumpstartYourInfluence.com and get access to the following now:

1. Jumpstart Yourself as a Speaker Audio Training

2. Jumpstart Yourself as an Author Webinar Training

3. Jumpstart Your Marketing Basics 3-Part Webinar Training

4. And an opportunity to have a Free Coaching Call with me!

Here's to creating a better world for us and our families!

About the Author
Katrina Sawa

Katrina Sawa is an award-winning international speaker and business coach known as the JumpStart Your Biz Coach, because she kicks her clients and their businesses into high gear! She is the creator of the JumpStart Your Marketing® System, Jumpstart Your Business System, and Int'l Best-Selling Author with 11 books. She loves to inspire and educate other entrepreneurs on how to create a consistent money-making business doing what they love.

Jumpstart Your Networking

Finding Leads and Building Relationships in Person, Virtually, and Online

By Katrina Sawa

Networking is one of my favorite ways to market myself and my business! Most people, I find, either love it or they hate it. But no matter how you slice it, networking for business connections, leads, and referrals can be your fastest path to cash!

I'm going to share tips about how to maximize your networking in person, on virtual networking events, by phone, and on social media.

Perfecting my networking has singularly impacted my business with more clients, more opportunities, more exposure, and more fun than any other part of the business plan.

Before you start networking, there are a few things to think about:

1. Have you defined your target market? Are you sure? Who is your ideal client?

2. Do you know where they hang out? Where can you find them in person or online, exactly? You need to start a list of places, events, conferences, social media platforms, groups, etc. Are they stay-at-home moms, who spend the majority of their time at their children's school events or sports? Do those places have meetings? Are they homeowners who might attend home shows or community meetings? Are they all realtors? Are you attending their monthly association meetings?

3. I recommend making a habit of attending one larger conference or 2-4-day event every quarter, at least. Locally, you can attend anywhere from 1-4 smaller events per week in most areas if you look hard enough. All the people you meet may not be exact prospects, but you might find prospects, referral sources, opportunities to be a speaker, and other opportunities you wouldn't have found otherwise.

4. What are your networking goals in the first place? To get clients? Speaking gigs? Sell? Make friends? Build your database? Find some good referral sources? Identify your goals so that you're focused.

5. You want to prepare yourself for networking. Schedule the events you'll attend on your calendar every month (make sure you're consistent, and go back to the ones that are good). Schedule time on

your calendar to do social media networking, too. That could take just 30 minutes per day, or you could do a bunch in one sitting if you want.

6. Practice your 30-60-second commercial, and have a couple variations available just in case.

7. Bring marketing materials in person, or have webpages ready for sharing when online.

During networking events, here are a few tips on how to maximize your time and have a clear strategy for "working the room":

1. Arrive early or on time, and allow enough time after the event for continued networking.

2. Be prepared to give advice, resources, and support to others--not just to talk about yourself.

3. Ask lots of questions of those you meet. People trust you more when you seem genuinely interested in them. Whenever you are nervous or not sure what to say to break the ice, ask a question.

4. Sometimes, you will also want to be an exhibitor or sponsor of an event--not just an attendee. This will give you additional exposure and an opportunity to showcase what you do.

5. Ask for people's business cards so you can follow up later, or schedule the "get-to-know-ya" type of a call right then and there. If you never get to that follow up call, you probably won't get the business.

6. You have to work the room. Don't talk to any one person too long. Try to learn as much as you can about them and get their contact information, and

move on. You have to do more than just hand out your information. Don't trust others to follow up; you have to be the one to make sure it happens.

7. Get the "verbal opt in." Ask them if they would like to receive more information and emails from you, and for those who say yes, add them to your database.

8. Create a Cheat Sheet. Write a list of all the key things you need to remember to talk about while you are networking. Read it before you go into the event or take it in if you need it--there's nothing wrong with that. I always have a list of the top three things I want to talk about when I go to a networking event, because my goals are always changing.

9. Don't just talk about what you DO; remember to ASK for what you NEED!

When networking on social media, here are a few tips on how to come off as more friendly and non-salesy:

1. When you click onto Facebook or LinkedIn, you have *billions* of people with whom you could potentially network--but you might feel more comfortable keeping to a small circle instead of reaching out to NEW people and prospects. It's like going to a live networking event or conference and just standing there, not talking to anyone... you wouldn't do that in person, right? Take the opportunity to branch out--it could really pay off.

2. As you're sending people Facebook friend requests or asking people to "LIKE" your business page, keep in mind that you would never just walk up

to someone at a live event, take out your business card, toss it at them, and walk away.

3. Send private messages, similar to what you'd say if you met them in person. You can do this with people who are connected to others you know, in groups to which you belong, or to people who just seem interesting. It's all about what you say in those messages--however, be careful. Don't send too many messages in one day; Facebook frowns on that.

When networking on virtual calls, meetings, and video events, here are a few tips on how to "work the virtual room":

1. I'm finding that, if I can substitute virtual networking for some of my in-person networking for which I have to travel, it takes less of a toll on my body, my family, my time, and my budget. And I'm finding that it works just as well!

2. First of all, the type of virtual call I'm talking about is NOT a typical webinar. A typical webinar involves someone getting on and teaching something, giving a presentation, or doing a signature talk. Usually webinars end with an offer of some sort. These are fine, but you normally can't "NETWORK" on a webinar. I'm talking about holding a call on a video platform, such as Zoom. Why a Video Platform? Because it's the closest thing to an in-person networking event that you can get – you can "see and feel" everyone's energy. You can also "talk to each person" in the "chat room," exchanging contact info and taking the relationship pretty quickly to a phone conversation or email exchange to begin the relationship-building process. The calls that

are focused on networking with all participants are the best, and they happen all the time.

3. These virtual calls are especially good when everyone gets a chance to introduce themselves first, and share what they do. Then you can be very specific about why you want to connect with the others on the call, and expedite the connecting process by giving them your online calendar scheduling link in the chat room. People book appointments with me *during* the call when I do this! I attend, speak on, or host approximately 8 to 40 of these virtual calls per month right now – and I get paying clients from them pretty quickly! *YOU CAN DO THIS TOO!!*

And finally, after the networking event or activity, how will you follow up? I have a really thorough system for Jumpstarting Your Follow-Up, and there's a chapter in this book about it too. Here are a few tips:

1. Make Sure You Always Follow Up Like Crazy. This is where most business owners fall short and don't actually maximize their time from networking in the first place. Most sales will be made on the follow-up. Most opportunities for speaking gigs or joint ventures will be made on the follow-up.

2. Calling to follow up is the best strategy, but you also want to follow up via email and direct mail, too. If you really want to make a big impression or get to someone quickly and they're not responding, then search them out on your favorite social media site and send them a message there, too.

3. One tip about follow-up is to NOT add everyone you meet to your email newsletter or a subscription

via email; that is spamming, and it is not good etiquette. If someone asks you to send them your information or be added to your list, then of course you can oblige.

4. Finally, you want to follow up more than one time in each way. Try a minimum of 2 direct mail attempts, emails, and phone calls for the best chance of response. Develop an easy follow-up system you can follow each week, or delegate it to an assistant so it gets done!

Whether you are comfortable networking or not, networking is a skill that you can learn. Practice and you'll get better at it.

I hope you're inspired to get out there and network in person or online. **If you are looking for some free resources or inexpensive training** on how to be as effective as you can while networking, as well as where to network, I have some resources for you. **Go to www.JumpstartYourNetworking.com and get access to the following:**

- Networking Checklist and Top 20 Networking Tips

- Video Conference Etiquette Checklist

- List of Online Networking Meetings, Calls, and Events Anyone Can Attend

If you're a small business owner looking to grow your business fast, then get networking!

About the Author
Katrina Sawa

Katrina Sawa is an award-winning international speaker and business coach known as the JumpStart Your Biz Coach, because she kicks her clients and their businesses into high gear! She is the creator of the JumpStart Your Marketing® System, Jumpstart Your Business System, and Int'l Best-Selling Author with 11 books. She loves to inspire and educate other entrepreneurs on how to create a consistent money-making business doing what they love.

Jumpstart Your Purpose

You'll Know It When You Feel It

By Dave Grill

Tuesday, August 4, 1981, I was sitting in the players' locker room dining area two days before the start of the 63rd PGA Championship at Atlanta Athletic Club. Two fellow competitors and I had finished our final day of practice and would be competing in the National Long Drive Championship the following morning, which was always held the day before the PGA Championship back in those days. As we were having a drink, waiting for our food order, a lone gentleman sauntered into the lounge area and immediately headed over to our table with a rather stern look on his face. Without introduction, the gentleman unapologetically asked the three of us, "Hey, what are you guys doing in my locker room?" I was quick to explain that we were there for the Long Drive Competition the next day, and as contestants, we had locker room privileges. He then gave us a big grin and chuckled as he pulled out the empty chair and sat down at the table while informing us that "If they would have had a long drive competition back when I was your age, I'd have won every year, because I could hit the ball a country mile back then."

As he was settling into his chair, the waiter arrived and asked, "Your regular, Mr. Palmer?" Mr. Palmer replied, "Yes, and why don't you bring me half a turkey sandwich and a side of potato salad too." It was on that day I discovered that an Iced Tea/ Lemonade mixture is a very refreshing drink, and that Arnold Palmer was every bit the gracious, down-to-earth gentleman I had always heard he was. After the Long Drive competition, I got my first taste of caddying on the PGA Tour for John Fought, 1979 PGA Rookie-of-the-year and older brother to my best friend from Portland, Oregon.

I learned a lot that week in Atlanta. My biggest take away: the life of a traveling PGA tour golfer is not what I had imagined, and living that lifestyle was certainly not my purpose.

Life purpose consists of all the central motivating factors in your life, the reason you get out of bed in the morning. Purpose can offer a sense of direction, influence behavior, shape goals, and guide life decisions.

Returning home to Portland from Atlanta, I was preparing for fall term at Lewis & Clark College in Portland, Oregon. It was there that I began to formulate and realize my purpose for living. Until that time, I had no idea what my purpose for being on this planet was. It would change from season to season, but I really did not have a true passion or purpose that I could really sink my teeth into.

I always thought my purpose would have something to do with sports. I had always excelled in sports, yet I never had that deep heartfelt passion for one sport over another. At Lewis & Clark College, I played football and golf--not your typical blend of athletic endeavors, but they were my two passions. Notice I said "passions," not "purpose." I LOVED football, yet I knew that my size and speed would not be something NFL scouts would salivate over. I really enjoyed golf, but I lacked the desire, discipline, and dedication to become extraordinarily good at it.

Then, spring term 1982, I found my purpose. I walked into my "Intro to Interpersonal Communication" class, sat down, and across the classroom, there sat my purpose: Teresa O'Brien. I stared at her for over a week until she finally approached me after class one day and introduced herself. From that day forward, we were inseparable, and we were married August 4th, 1984.

For me, I found my purpose in Teresa, and in trying to be the best husband I could be for her. In 1986, we were blessed with our first child, Nicole. She expanded my purpose, as I was now trying to be the best husband and parent I could be. 1988 and 1990 brought two more wonderful children, Lauren and John. Life was grand, and my purpose in life was completely solidified. This family was the reason I got out of bed in the morning.

Teresa and I were very much on the same page regarding raising the kids. They were involved in all kinds of activities, including sports, drama, and music. Teresa was a middle school teacher, which allowed her to be home with the kids during the summer, school breaks, and holidays. Our careers allowed us to coach the kids' teams in a variety of sports, and our lives revolved around their activities and family functions. We tried to instill in them many of the values our parents instilled in us, such as:

- The importance of family

- Belief in yourself

- Don't worry about what others think of you

- Be a leader, not a follower

- Life will knock you down, but you must always get back up

- Don't be a victim

- Never, ever quit

We allowed the kids to try different things they thought would be interesting, but with one caveat: if they started it, they had to finish it.

By 1998, our lives were a blur, rushing from one kid activity to another. Both of our careers were going well. Teresa was still teaching and moving into more of an administrative role at her middle school, looking towards obtaining her Master's Degree and becoming a principal, *her purpose on this planet.* My career in the scrap metal recycling business was on virtual autopilot, as I had successfully built a consistent base of repeat customers month in, month out.

Returning home from a business trip to southern Oregon in September, Teresa greeted me with a concerned look on her face. She had discovered an unusual lump on the side of her breast, just below her armpit. The lump turned out to be malignant, and she underwent grueling chemotherapy and extensive radiation treatments over the course of the next several months. By the early part of 1999, her doctors were confident that the treatments had been successful, and she was deemed to be cancer free. To say that this event was difficult on everyone in the family would be an understatement, yet in many ways, it brought the family closer together. We were all very thankful that it was over, and life could return to some semblance of normalcy. After recovering from her ordeal, Teresa enrolled into the Master's Program at George Fox University to begin taking the next step toward becoming a principal. Life was returning to normal. The kids were all involved in sports and school activities, we were blessed, and life was good. We may have been knocked down, but we were all back up and running again.

The summer of 2000 found the entire family following our middle daughter Lauren's little league softball team that I was coaching, as they qualified for the Little League World Series. There were numerous qualifying tournaments culminating in late August after losing the Championship game to a team from Waco, Texas. It was an exhilarating experience even for the two other siblings, who really got into cheering on their sister throughout the summer. Most of the parents were thoroughly exhausted, and had to face getting kids ready for back-to-school in a couple of weeks. Teresa had been totally wrapped up in all the excitement of the World Series and, after its conclusion, finally admitted to feeling a bit run-down...and she was experiencing some unusual abdominal discomfort. She checked in with her doctors, but they attributed it to all the excitement and activity. By mid-September, her pain and discomfort had increased, and she went in for a complete check-up. The cancer had returned with a vengeance to her liver and other organs. We lost her on November 25th, 2000. Before her death, Teresa asked me to promise that the kids and I would go on and be happy. I made her that promise, even though I had no idea how that would be possible.

I am proud to say that, nearly twenty years later, Nicole, Lauren, and John are thriving and have given me and my wife, Kellie Poulsen-Grill, six beautiful grandchildren. This past April, Kellie and I celebrated our 18th wedding anniversary. She stepped in when the kids were 10, 12, and 14 years old, and she and our family continue to be my purpose in this crazy, wonderful, beautiful life. Ironically, I left my 25-year career March 1st, 2019, after I invented The Delta Putt, a golf putting training device. I don't drive it as far now, but I have never putted better.

The Delta Putt is an amazing device. If you know any golfers out there, I invite you to send them to my website for more information at www.DeltaPutt.com. **You can also go and grab my FREE Download: "Seven Tips to Improving your Putting," if you go to this special page just for you: www.DeltaPutt. com/jumpstart.**

Finally, I hope you take whatever steps you can to go find your purpose, and don't settle for less!

About the Author
Dave Grill

Dave Grill, "The Dave," is an Inventor, Author, Speaker, Songwriter, Businessman, and all-around great athlete. Dave has always excelled in sports, playing Baseball, Football, Hockey, and Golf. In 2016, he invented his golf training aid, "The Delta Putt," and opened his company GSIX Products, where he holds 3 patents. Dave is married to Kellie Grill, and together they have 3 children, 6 grandchildren, and 30 animals--12 of which are horses.

Jumpstart Your YouTube Channel

How to Set Up and Start Attracting Clients And Followers on YouTube

By Nate Anderson

Did you know that YouTube has become the second largest social media platform, only behind Facebook? It would be a disservice for your business to not focus on YouTube as a method of building it up. Although making videos and running a channel can seem daunting, it's a very straightforward process, once you get into it.

I started my YouTube channel in 2015 at age 13. I wanted to get creative and start developing content. Through this process, I have discovered a love for creating and editing videos, as well as storytelling through videos. Since I started, I have been able to grow my channel, Galactic Hole, to over 60,000 subscribers. Don't get intimidated by this, though-- you can do it too!

One quick warning is to pay attention to your channel's security. YouTube hasn't always gone smoothly for me, as I had my channel hacked in February of 2020. The hackers started uploading spam political content, which cost me around 7,000 subscribers. It took me three months to finally get the channel back in my hands. That process was made even more difficult due to the lack of communication YouTube and Google provided through their customer support. Ultimately, I had to reach out using the connections I've made to be able to speak with someone who worked at YouTube, just to fix the problem. Channel security is incredibly important, and I recommend implementing it before you get started. Make sure you have all of the security measures for your email turned on, including two-factor authentication and backup phone number and email. Never open emails that seem fishy and involve your channel potentially being shut down, or include fake brand offers. Doing those two easy steps will keep your channel in your own hands and allow you to continue growing your online presence.

YouTube is a tricky market in which to grow your business, but if done right, it can lead to great success. All of the opportunities I have received have been because of my work through YouTube, and you will have the best shot at achieving that same success through following the steps laid out in this chapter.

First of all, the part that comes easy to me (and may not to you) is what content to develop. What are you an expert in? What advice can you give? I'll bet you have articles or interviews or even other types of content in your head about what's important to share with your ideal prospects. Share that. You don't want to overthink this; just keep track of your ideas and get them out.

Recording and Editing Videos

We're not perfect. We make mistakes when we talk. Maybe we want our video to be a bit flashier to attract more people and keep their attention for longer. Video editing is definitely the most difficult step to getting your business on YouTube, but there are free tools to help you out.

- **HitFilm Express**

HitFilm Express is the best overall free editing software. It works great for simple edits, such as trimming out unwanted sections, as well as more advanced edits, such as adding effects and animation to clips. The software is easy to get into and will hold up for more adventurous edits later on down the road.

- **iMovie**

iMovie is the most widely used video editing software for Mac users, and it is a great program with which to start. You can add themes and video effects to your videos very easily, although it lacks some of the more advanced features that some editors may want in order to make their videos look very professional. iMovie even has a feature to upload your videos directly to YouTube, making the process even smoother.

- **DaVinci Resolve**

DaVinci is a fantastic program for those who want more advanced features in a free package. Most edits are very simple and intuitive, although there is a learning curve for the more advanced edits the program can handle. It is recommended that you start with one of the previously mentioned programs if you are completely new to editing.

Uploading and Using YouTube for Business

YouTube is a great platform on which to share education and act as a figure for people to look up to. You can give tutorials, share practices, and anything else that individuals who are looking for your business might find valuable. Most searches start with "How to," so it is a wise decision to do the same for your videos in order to draw in the most people. Uploading frequent, informative, and high-quality content to your channel will give you the best chance at attracting viewers and potential business. Keeping up an online presence with appealing thumbnails and titles will increase your chances of building an audience on YouTube, but don't be too discouraged if you aren't receiving the success you first expected. YouTube is a huge platform with 300 hours of video uploaded every minute, and not all of this content can get recommended for everyone to see.

Tracking Engagement

Once you have videos up and are starting to gain a following, you can track your videos' engagement in many ways. By going to your YouTube studio page (click on your profile picture, and then click on "YouTube Studio"), you can immediately see how your latest video has performed in comparison to the previous ones in terms of views, view duration, and the rate of people clicking through to your other videos. On the left side of the Studio page, you can click on the Analytics tab to see more in-depth features. From here, you can check how your amount of views, watch time, subscribers, and revenue have progressed over the last 28 days. There are lots of different features here that you can check over to see how your channel has been doing recently, or since its creation.

Monetization

It sounds great to be able to monetize your YouTube channel, but you definitely won't be using it as a main source of income. You will need a base level of 1,000 subscribers total and 4,000 watch hours over the last 12 months to enable monetization. What this means is that your channel needs to have 4,000 hours that other people have watched of your content over the last calendar year. Livestreams on the channel count towards these 4,000 hours, but if you delete a video, the total time others have watched that video will be removed from this count.

Apply - Once you reach these requirements, you will need to go to your YouTube Studio page and then to the Monetization tab on the left side. From here, you can apply into the YouTube Partner Program. It will take a few weeks, as a real person will have to review your channel, but you will then receive either a rejection or acceptance into the program. If you get rejected, make sure your channel follows all of the YouTube Community Guidelines on content, and then reapply.

Approved - When you have been approved, you now have to create an AdSense account that will be connected with your bank. Go to Google.com/ AdSense, click "Get Started," and follow the steps to get set up.

How do ads get added to my videos?

Once you have the AdSense account connected with your channel, you can now apply ads to your videos. Going into your YouTube Studio page and clicking on the Videos tab, you can see all of your uploaded videos, which all have a new Monetization column. From here, you can simply click on the icon next to the video and switch it to "On." Your video will now be running ads on it. Videos that have monetization placed on them will get ads based on the viewers' browsing history, or based on the content of the video with similarly-themed ads. You do not get to choose which ads get placed in front of your content. Videos shorter than 10 minutes can only have an ad before the video, whereas videos longer than this can have ads placed in the middle of the video. When you upload a video, there will also be a new monetization step where you can turn ads on while you upload the video.

Payments - YouTube payments will be directly deposited to your bank account once a month, so long as your channel has earned at least $100. For some perspective on this, one million views typically translates to around $500, although specific numbers vary based on how often people click on your ads and how often the ads show on your videos.

When to Hire Help

Hiring a videographer and video editor may be the step you need to take if you do not have the time to edit your videos. It's worth it to hire someone to make your content look as professional as possible, as you want to make an excellent first impression on the online world. **If you would like to get my FREE Download, Top 5 Video Editing Tips, or if you are looking for additional information, go to www.DynamicVideo.me/jumpstart.**

About the Author
Nate Anderson

Nathan (Nate) Anderson is a recent high school graduate. It was during high school when he found his passion for video editing and creating mashup videos at an early age. Self-taught on Premiere Pro and other video editing software, he has grown his YouTube channel to over 60,000 subscribers. In his spare time, Nate loves to create and listen to music, weightlift, and skateboard.

What's Next?

What did you think of the stories and expertise that our authors had to share?

Did you learn a few new things to take back to your life or work?

My hope is that you did learn a few things, or at least walk away with a fresh new way of thinking about some of our topics. If so, please go over to Amazon and leave us a review! Make sure you choose the "orange" colored *Jumpstart Your* _____ book as there are two others there.

Our authors have been hand-selected due to their level of expertise, genuine integrity, and overall skill level in their industry. If you enjoyed reading some of their stories or learning more about how they help their clients, please take the next step and reach out to those who spoke to you.

Most of the authors in this book speak to groups of all sizes, both in person and virtually. They also offer products, programs, events, and services that can support you in one or more areas of your life, health, or business / career.

I highly recommend that you take advantage of their special offers, additional downloads, and more when you visit each of the websites listed at the end of their chapters.

In addition, I've put together ONE page on my website where you can access all of the Jumpstart Author's websites and special offers, to make it easy for you to follow up. **Go to www.JumpstartBookAuthors. com** right now, before you forget who you wanted to connect with or find out more about. All authors from all Jumpstart books are on that page.

Thank you for reading this book, and I look forward to bringing you more Jumpstart Your _____ Authors in upcoming books, plus more training and teachings in my own books.

If you are an author who has something that YOU help people JUMPSTART and you would like to be considered as one of our next Jumpstart Authors, please go to www.JumpstartPublishing.net now and apply!

WHAT DO YOU HELP YOUR CLIENTS JUMPSTART?

In the *Jumpstart Your* _____ book series, YOU Fill in the Blank with the thing YOU do with YOUR clients for YOUR chapter, and become an author this year! Use this book as a MARKETING TOOL to get leads and grow your business.

Interested in becoming an author easily?

Get into a compilation book of 15-20 authors and write ONE chapter, but get huge exposure for you and your business, along with every author promoting it alongside you! Attract new clients and make more money after your prospects are introduced to you in this book.

Want to get more exposure, speaking gigs, or clients in the coming year? Become an author!

While it could take a while for you to write your own full book, it's relatively easy to get published in an anthology or compilation book by just writing one chapter. Everyone in the book promotes the books and sells them, so you get in front of a lot more people than you would with just your own book. PLUS... we do all the work! **Find out how this could benefit you here:**

www.JumpstartPublishing.net.

ABOUT KATRINA SAWA
CEO OF K. SAWA MARKETING
INT'L INC.
AND JUMPSTART PUBLISHING

Katrina Sawa is known as the Jump-Start Your Biz Coach because she literally kicks her clients and their businesses into high gear, online & offline, and fast. Katrina is the creator of the JumpStart Your Marketing® System, Jump-Start Your Business System, Jumpstart Yourself as a Speaker System. She is an International Best-Selling Author with 11 books. Katrina's first, hosted anthology book, *Jumpstart Your _____* was published in Fall of 2018 and now every year Kat gets to help 12-20 entrepreneurs become authors as a new volume of *Jumpstart Your ____* is published annually.

Katrina helps entrepreneurs make smarter marketing and business decisions in order to create the life and business of your dreams. She helps you create your big picture vision, plan and initial offerings if you're just starting out. She helps you develop a more leveraged, efficient business and marketing plan if you're more seasoned. Either way, she shows you all the steps, systems and marketing that need to be put in place in order to accomplish your big picture business, life and money goals. She does this via one-on-one coaching, her Live Big Mastermind, her Live Big Events, Webinars, Podcasts, and numerous Facebook groups she runs.

Katrina is the founder of the International Entrepreneur Network and CEO of the International Speaker Network. She won the National Collaborator of the Year Award by the Public Speakers Association of who's conference which Katrina spoke for four years in a row. She is also a member of the Women's Speaker Association, eWomenNetwork, Women's Prosperity Network and a Diamond Member of Polka Dot Powerhouse. Kat speaks to groups and conferences of all sizes all over North America and the Internet.

One thing that makes Katrina different is that she also focuses on her clients' personal lives. She found that most business owners lack enough self-confidence to truly enable them to get to their next level, or take those leaps of faith they need to achieve their ultimate dreams. Katrina's goal is to inspire, motivate, and educate entrepreneurs on how to love themselves fully, live a bigger life, and leverage themselves to complete happiness.

Katrina has a degree in Business Administration, Marketing Concentration, from California State University Sacramento, and has been a featured business expert on three of her local television news channels throughout her career thus far.

Katrina lives in Northern California with her husband Jason, step-daughter Riley, and their German Shepherd, Willow.

You can find out all about Kat and her products, programs, services, and live events online at www.JumpstartYourBizNow.com or www. JumpstartPublishing.net.

Motivate and Inspire Others!
"Share this Book"

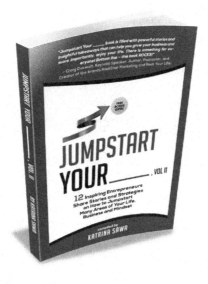

Retail $16.95 + Tax & Shipping

Special Quantity Discounts

5 - 15 Books	**$11.95 Each**
16 - 30 Books	**$9.95 Each**
30 - 1,000 Books	**$7.95 Each**

To Place an Order Contact:

K. Sawa Marketing International Inc.
916-872-4000

info@JumpstartYourBizNow.com
or go to www.JumpstartPublishing.net

Grab One or More of the Jumpstart Your Business Free Trainings Now!

Learn How to:

- Get Started Speaking

- Jumpstart Your Business

- Implement Best Marketing Practices

- Build an Effective

- Website

- Create a Life You Love

- Find Your Purpose

- Love Yourself Successful

- Delegate & Build Your Team

- And more!

Get Access Online at: www. JumpstartYourBizNow.com/ FreeTrainings

Want a Deeper Training on How to Start, Grow, Market & Monetize Your Business?

- In Depth Training, How-To, Templates
- Roadmap & Plan to Jumpstart Your Biz
- Hot Seat Coaching
- Learn from Topic Specific Speakers
- Mastermind & Network
- Make Money with Easy YES Offers

Attend One of Kat's Live Events! Get Information at www.LiveBigEvents.com

Book Katrina to Speak:

K. Sawa Marketing International Inc.
PO Box 6, Roseville, CA 95661
916-872-4000 | info@JumpstartYourBizNow.com
www.JumpstartYourBizNow.com/speaking

Made in USA - Kendallville, IN
1186887_9781735866611
10.28.2020 0838